GHOSTS

of the

FOX RIVER

VALLEY

by Donna Latham

Dedication

To my husband Nick, the touchstone

And

To all those who came before us to settle the beautiful Fox River Valley—and whose spirits never left it.

Preface

Most of us have skeletons in our closets. Some of us also have ghosts. I grew up in a haunted house, and I know that I'm not the only person who's experienced fidgety spirits. In addition, I live in scenic St. Charles. In fact, I often pass the historic building where, legend has it, the grieving widow Mary Todd Lincoln visited a medium to contact the spirits of her departed husband and son.

My riverfront town is proud of its rich history. That history includes secret stations on the Underground Railroad with tunnels and false entryways; the 18th Regiment, which trained at Camp Kane and later, took part in the gory battle of Gettysburg; and even a messy mob incident incited by a grave robber.

I let it be known that I was writing ghost stories set in the Fox River Valley from Waukesha to Oswego—locations with their own vivid histories. I announced that the stories covered the period from the mid-1800's to the present. Quickly, friends, neighbors, and friends of friends came forward to reveal their own experiences, many for the first time. Almost all those who spoke to me were certain they had encountered folks who were not quite ready to give up the ghost. Dead certain.

Several the tales people shared struck a familiar chord; perhaps those fall into the realm of ghostlore, which gets passed around like so much pocket change. Often, it was only an anecdote or a snippet that people related; these I fleshed into longer tales.

Other yarns were strictly known to only a few people; their tellers requested anonymity, so these stories use fictitious names. It should be understood that any similarity between those names and actual persons, living or dead, is purely coincidental. In fact, while this collection mentions historical people and relates pieces of history, it remains a work of fiction.

These stories are not of the blood 'n' guts ilk (although "Old Blood and Guts" Patton figures into one of them) or those with a religious stance. Instead, they are simply tales of ghosts that have lingered in the Fox River Valley.

I'd like to express my immense gratitude to my husband Nick Longo, my brother Bill Latham, and my friend Judy Nayer, who read my manuscript in its incubating stages. In addition, I'd like to thank the libraries and historical museums of the Fox River Valley. Their collections are truly treasure troves.

The Train Track Ghosts

When Wilbur Hawkings heard that I was collecting ghost stories, he paid me one of his occasional calls. I look forward to his visits as much for the yarns he spins as for the reassurance of his laughter.

Wilbur eased his lanky frame into my rocker. His mischievous eyes peered out from a face marked by as many lines as Illinois' railroads. In an easy silence, we watched the great blue herons fishing outside my cottage along the Fox River. I live in St. Charles, the town known as "the Pride of the Fox."

"I was what you'd dub a train tramp back in the Great Depression," Wilbur began, gently rocking. "I was only 15. Didn't weigh but a buck twenty. Wet behind the ears, I was. The older hoboes showed me the ropes. Recollectin' it now, I just shake my head in awe at the risks I took. Imagine hoppin' a ten-ton speeding iron monster as it thundered down the tracks."

"I can't imagine it," I shuddered.

"Those were dark days in our history, they were," Wilbur continued. "But I'm an optimistic sort—have to be at my age, or what's the alternative?" Wilbur smacked his bony knee and chuckled. "I prefer to recall the adventure. Not the hardship."

"It's an attitude that's served you well," I said. "That's obvious by those twinkling eyes. More coffee?"

"You betcha," he said. Griping his steaming cup, Wilbur grew contemplative for a moment. He stared out the window, swaying.

"All those years I spent crossin' the Midwest on locomotives, searchin' high and low for wages and a place to hang my hat … Doesn't it figure I'd finally meet up with those ol' train track ghosts that haunt Wayne?"

Wayne is a rural equestrian community with a population of just over 2,100. In the winters, without the shroud of protective foliage, you can glimpse the town's famous Dunham Castle, a French chateau's doppelgänger. Elsewhere in the village, stately Wayne manors and stables sprawl across considerable acreage.

Wildlife flourishes in Wayne's protected wetlands. Horses abound—and bound. It's not unusual, as you zoom across woodsy Dunham Road, to pass leaping horses. Each year, the bucolic community reenacts a traditional foxhunt—with a fox-friendly twist. Rather than foxes, hounds pursue trails left by drag bags, which emit fox scents.

"I've heard about the train track ghosts," I said. "Legend has it that a woman's car stalled on the tracks."

"Yep," said Wilbur. "She warned her kids to stay in the car. Then she hopped out to peer under the hood. Got so engrossed in what she was doing, that she didn't hear the train approach—and she and her kids died on those tracks."

For a moment, we were silent. We listened to the creak of the rocking chair.

"Tell me, Wilbur, about your experiences," I said.

"As much as it gives my daughter conniptions, I still drive every single day," Wilbur began. "Keeps me independent. Got a nice routine. Head downtown to grab a cuppa Joe and a plate of scrambled eggs every mornin'. Then I stop off at the country store to buy my lottery ticket—like I say, I'm an optimist."

I smiled and passed the cookies.

"Appreciate it. Well, last February I made the grievous error of attempting to follow my usual routine after that wicked snowstorm. Crossing the train tracks, I got stuck in an icy snowdrift. Couldn't budge. I tried everything—layin' on the brakes, rockin' the car like I'm rockin' this chair. I even jammed a rubber floor mat under a tire to try to get some traction."

"My cousin taught me that trick back in the Blizzard of '79," I said. "Did it work?"

"No such luck. I just heard that relentless whir of my tires and felt the frigid wind rip right through me. Well, I had just resorted to prayin'—hard—when I heard the train blast its horn. For an instant, I was just like my car. Couldn't budge. I was prepared to meet my Maker right then and there. Always figured, as a train tramp, that a locomotive would do me in. I guess I was kinda prepared, in an odd way."

Again he gazed out the window.

"Well, ma'am, the darndest thing happened next. Felt like little hands were yankin' on my coat, draggin' me to the trunk of the car. I reeled around and there they were. Two little tow-headed boys, dressed for summer in shorts and sandals. One boy pressed his hands against the bumper. The other laid his right near the trunk's keyhole. They didn't speak a word, but they sure did communicate with me—'Push!'"

"So there, with that iron behemoth barrelin' toward us, I pushed with all my might. And with the help of those little tykes, I moved that car off the tracks—just in the nick of time. The wind from that thunderin' train blastin' past us knocked me right off my feet!"

"Did you find out who the boys were?"

"Well, m'dear, that's where the ghosts come in," Wilbur said. "Once the train passed, there was no trace of those kids—no sandal tracks in the snow, no nothin'. I thought I'd imagined them or that I'd gone off my—ah, rocker." Again, he slapped his knee merrily.

"But when I got home and pulled into the carport, I saw four little bitty handprints on my car. Two on the bumper. Two near the trunk's keyhole."

"Do you think the boys were the ghosts of the kids who died on the tracks?" I wondered.

"Yep, I sure do. I owe those two little ghost boys my life. Come on out to my car with me. I'll show you their handprints. Try though I might these months, I can't scrub 'em away."

We walked to the car. And there they were—four little handprints. In the swampy August heat, I shivered.

"What do you make of it, Wilbur?"

"I don't know what to make of it," he sighed. "But I sure do like seein' those little bitty prints. Kind of feels like I have angels on my shoulders. Call me an optimist."

The Flapper in the Fog

It was a mild winter evening in 1975. As usual, Juan Marino was running late.

An aspiring actor, Juan was putting himself through college in Lisle. He juggled a frenzied schedule. In the mornings, Juan was strictly in student mode. However, at noon, he dashed off campus to work at a little café over at the Morton Arboretum. Daily, he prayed that his wheezing two-seater would survive one more roundtrip.

When his shift ended, Juan zoomed back to campus. Most nights he spent onstage at rehearsals for the spring play. He hit the pillow long after midnight. By that time, Juan's eyelids seemed to be weighted down with oil drums.

If he ever had a fleeting moment to ponder his unexamined life—and he never did—Juan would have realized that he was lonely. Despite his hectic calendar and the many folks whose paths he crossed, Juan lacked a true companion to share life's journey.

This particular evening, as dusk fell, spring seemed within arm's reach, although it was officially a few weeks away. It was one of those misty March nightfalls—an unusually mild evening when winter was inclined to call a truce. The sky was not yet fully dark.

Zipping across an open country road, Juan checked his rearview mirror. He floored it. The last thing he needed was to be late for rehearsal. He cracked the window to enjoy the balmy breeze.

"What luck!" Juan muttered, observing a considerable patch of fog. It flitted across a curve in the road ahead. He flicked on his fog beams and decelerated. Cautiously, he rounded the bend.

Appearing out of nowhere, a young woman seemed to float on the fog. Startled, Juan wrenched the wheel and screeched to a halt. He felt the blood pulse in his temple. His heart beat a rowdy tattoo in his chest.

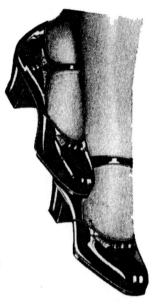

Juan launched from his car. "Are you OK?" he bellowed.

"Absolutely! I'm fine, honestly. I didn't see your jalopy until the last minute with all this fog."

Juan said, "Thank God I was able to stop. I could've killed you!"

"Yes, thank goodness," the woman replied. "Do you think I could I get a ride to the juice joint up the road? My dogs are killing me in these heels."

She daintily lifted a leg and showed Juan her shoe. It was an old-fashioned t-strapped number. Juan had seen similar ones in the theatre's wardrobe room.

The woman was dressed head to toe for a costume party, Juan noted, in a fuchsia satin flapper outfit. A black crocheted cap, festooned with swinging beads, framed her delicate face. A string of braided beads, silver and black, dangled nearly to her knees. She clutched a tiny beaded bag. The costume designer in Juan's drama department would kill for a vintage ensemble like that.

Juan's heart continued to race. Now, it was more from the presence of the ruby-lipped blonde than from his earlier close call. Juan held the passenger side door open as the woman climbed in. Then he ran around the car and jumped in.

"I'm Juan, by the way," he said. "Welcome to my—what did you call it? Ah, my *jalopy*. I prefer *beater* myself." He chuckled. "And you are—?"

"Elizabeth."

"Now, where did you say you were off to, Elizabeth?"

"The juice joint—up the road about ten miles."

Silently, Juan marveled at the fact that Elizabeth was traveling the distance on foot.

She said, "You know, the red brick building with the yellow awnings. It's not much to look at from the outside, but inside it's really swanky. The awnings are the cat's pajamas. You can't miss them."

Juan didn't know the place, but continued driving. He'd hit it sooner or later.

Elizabeth explained, "I'm meeting my girlfriend Sheila for a bit of giggle juice. We're putting on the Ritz tonight to celebrate her engagement."

"Well, if Sheila is decked out like you, it's going to be one heck of a party," Juan said.

Suddenly, Juan realized he had grown cold. He cranked up the window. Even when he flipped on the heat, he couldn't seem to stop shivering. Juan removed each hand in turn from the wheel and blasted it with a jet of his warm breath. Still, he felt as if some joker had dropped a block of ice down his back.

"Must have been that terrible fright Elizabeth gave me," he thought.

With mounting animation, Elizabeth chattered on. Although he was in close proximity, Juan scarcely listened to Elizabeth's words. Instead, he admired, in his actor's way, the music of her lilting voice, a voice brimming with limitless possibilities.

Juan valiantly attempted to keep his eyes on the road. Thankfully, the fog dissipated, so he could sneak an intermittent sideways glance Elizabeth's way. Gradually, he loosened up and entertained Elizabeth with witty anecdotes about his part in the play and his work as a cook.

"I'd be congratulating myself for being so smooth," Juan thought, "If I weren't trying to hide my frozen nose."

"There it is, Juan," cried Elizabeth, pointing. "There's the juice joint."

Reluctantly, Juan slowed his vehicle, which shuddered and coughed in response. He felt terribly drawn to Elizabeth—they had chemistry, as his director would say. Juan didn't want to see Elizabeth leave.

The "joint" was a bulky brick four-flat. On its façade, yellow awnings flapped garishly over arched windows.

"This is it? It looks like an old apartment building," cried Juan. "It's not what I expected…."

"Believe me, inside it's the bee's knees!"

The joint was hopping. Jazz music blared. A mint-condition Tin Lizzy pulled in next to Juan, its driver blasting the horn in greeting. *Ah-OO-ga!* Merrymakers, dressed in costumes like Elizabeth's, waved gleefully.

"How could I have missed a rockin' place like that?" Juan chided himself. "I've gotta stop and smell the roses every now and then."

"Juan, won't you join us? I've had such a lovely time with you—I don't want to see it end."

Time seemed to stand still as longing and duty battled. Juan was racing the clock. Rehearsal loomed. Yet, he and Elizabeth had clicked. He would never forgive himself for just driving away.

"I would love that, Elizabeth, really," Juan said, with extreme reluctance. "But I have to get to rehearsal or my director will have my head."

"What about afterwards? We'll be here 'til the crack of dawn."

"I'll be back by midnight," Juan promised. "You'll wait for me?"

"Absolutely!"

Shyly, Elizabeth reached for his hand.

"You're freezing," Juan cried. Her hand was like ice in his. He tucked it into the crook of his arm to warm it for a moment.

"See you later, alligator. Thanks for the ride."

When Juan slid regretfully back into the car, he noticed that Elizabeth's long beads had slipped to the floor. He grabbed them and prepared to sprint after her. Then he realized that she had left them on purpose to ensure his return. He was convinced. He forgot about his numb nose and sped toward campus.

After rehearsal Juan raced back to the joint, but he grew
disoriented in the inky night. He couldn't locate the precise
place where he had dropped off Elizabeth.

"I never should have let her go!" he thought. Inconsolable, he
returned the following morning. He found no sign of the
building on that day or on the frenzied days that followed.

In time, Juan learned there had once been a speakeasy on that
country road. It fell to the wrecker's ball in the early 1930's.
There is no trace of it today—and there shouldn't have been in
1975. Yet, he was certain he had seen its yellow awnings, had
heard its infectious music, had been entranced by one of its
revelers.

Nowadays, Juan is a member of a successful theatre troupe in
Chicago. He returns to that country road each March, just as
winter is about to relinquish its death grip on the Fox Valley.
Juan longs for a reunion with Elizabeth, but it hasn't come, yet.
In fact, if he didn't have Elizabeth's beads right there, right in
front of his eyes, draped 'round the mirror in his car, Juan
might be convinced that she had been an apparition—a ghostly
flapper in the fog.

Stage Presence

Places of extraordinary passion and creativity, theatres are especially alluring to ghosts. That spring evening in 1938, the alluring Ghost of Hamlet's father was on Lenore McClintock's mind.

Lenore religiously followed a pre-performance ritual. First, she applied her make-up in total silence. Then, she tucked a shiny new penny inside her shoe for luck. Finally, she planted a lipstick kiss on the mirror.

"Break a leg!" she cried, speaking aloud for the first time that day.

Such was Lenore's custom as a participant in an art fraught with superstitions. She was well aware that during a performance anything and everything could go wrong. Lest she curse the show, Lenore never whistled or clapped backstage. She, like all the other actors she knew, refused to utter the name of Shakespeare's "Scottish play," dreading the catastrophic consequences that might befall the theatre or its players.

Lenore had won the prized role of Ophelia in *Hamlet*, Shakespeare's grueling, intricate tragedy. Like many, she considered the lengthy play to be Shakespeare's finest work. Lenore felt honored to be cast.

Lithe and lively, Lenore tiptoed backstage to observe her boyfriend, Ted Waldman, make his entrance. Portraying the Ghost of Hamlet's father, Ted wore a ghastly gray mask and headpiece, which made him tower to seven feet. In a swirling mist released from a trap door, he materialized and seized the stage. No matter how many times Lenore witnessed the effect, it never ceased to thrill her, to send a shiver down her spine.

A second ghost rose from the mist. This one loomed above Ted and drifted overhead. Shrouded in a colorless garment with billowing wizard's sleeves, he dramatically emoted, providing an eerie echo of Ted's lines. Shakespeare's immortal words reverberated through the house.

"I am thy father's spirit,
Doom'd for a certain term to walk the night."

The effect was chilling. The audience was riveted. They breathed as one and clung to the resounding words.

Lenore was stunned. Her arms dangled limply at her sides. For you see, gentle reader, this second specter was unknown and uninvited.

When the dual ghosts exited, the audience burst into the spontaneous applause that sparingly honors especially laudable performers. Ted strode offstage into the mist. Waving his billowing sleeves, Ted's ghost partner exited over the house. The delighted audience roared in approval.

Backstage, Ted hissed. "Get me out of this headpiece!" Released, he was as ashen as the mask. "What the—? Who was—? Did you—?"

The actors nodded solemnly. No one likes to be upstaged, especially by a scenery-chewing phantom. Ted was no exception.

Who was the ghostly thespian? Perhaps a player of the past, fluttering in for one final performance.... Today, actors who perform in that historic theatre, whose location I have vowed to keep confidential, speak often of the supernatural—and legendary—performance. All agree that it was no garden-variety phantom that seized the stage with Ted so long ago.

Nowadays, actors hear persistent whisperings in the catwalks above the stage. Mysterious footsteps echo behind them in the wardrobe room. When actors slip into their costumes, the clothing feels warm, as if someone has just removed it.

Yet, the spectral performer has yet to tread the boards again. Instead, he sits among the audience in his favorite seat. Front and center. Actors swear they can feel his presence; a cold draft fills the house when he comes to call. They maintain that they hear the phantom whisk in just as the curtain rises. He pulls down his seat and settles with a *whoosh* into the velvet cushion. Audience members claim they have sat beside the taciturn spectator, who evaporates before the curtain call.

For their part, actors leave modest offerings of gum and chocolate on the seat's armrest to entice the ghost to remain seated. After the performances, these sweets are invariably gone and the players relieved.

As I explained, gentle reader, actors are extremely superstitious. And one can scarcely blame them.

Hanging Around the Boys' Gym

This story came to me by way of a high school
custodian from Aurora. He selected the
pseudonym Flip Kuhlman and the generic school
name Giant High School to assure anonymity. In
a cramped backhand, Flip wrote his story for me
on yellow legal paper. This caveat opened his
work: "Feel free to fix up my writing any way
you see fit. Use writerly words and whatnot. I'm
good with my hands. I'm only so-so with
words."

I disagree. Flip's story follows, verbatim.

I've been prowling every nook and cranny of Giant H.S. for
going on 35 years now. I promise you, I've seen (and smelled) it
all. Malodorous explosions in the chemistry labs. A dazed
possum that somehow wandered into the cafeteria on pizza day.
Long-lost sandwiches that turn up in freshman lockers—so
moldy they probably hold the cure for some disease. And even a
misguided senior prank involving a Volkswagen and the library.
(Don't ask.) Man, could I keep you up for hours with my
stories. But I digress.

Me, I just slap on my poker face, mind my own beeswax, and
do my job. I've always worked the day shift, except for a little
stretch in my first year at Giant. Right after I started there in
1971, the custodian who works nights—let's call him
Jesse—started complaining about odd goings-on.
Strange sounds and such. I didn't pay much attention. That
Jesse. He's a bit of a whiner.

But when he threw his back out and went on medical leave, I had to pull a few double shifts. Then I learned exactly what he meant.

It was around midnight. The school was spooky-silent. Now, that's real unusual. Ordinarily, I hear cracks and rattles and wheezes and whatnot. The sounds of a school trying to get a good night's sleep before the galloping marauders invade in the morning. That night was different. Creeped me out, like my daughter would say. Then I got a whiff of a horrid odor—worst I've ever smelled.

The building was dead empty, except for two guys. One was me, way over in the upper level of the boys' gym. The other was the night watchman—let's call him Collins. He was way, way up at the main entry. I called him on my walkie-talkie.

"Yo, Collins. Anything out of the ordinary up there? Over."

"Nope. Quiet as a tomb," Collins replied. "How's by you? Over."

"Stinks to high heaven in the boys' gym. Over."

"'Course it does. It's a *boys' gym!* Over."

"Funny, Collins, fun-nee. Over and out."

I decided to investigate. Suddenly, from the basketball court on the lower level, I heard a squeak. It was unmistakable—that screech that athletic shoes make as they hustle around the court. Hear it all the time when I watch Bulls games—which aren't nearly as fun anymore without Jordan. But I digress.

I stood shock still and listened. I heard that squeak again, followed by the *boom, boom, boom* of a dribbled ball. Then came a *twack* of the ball against the backstop.

I hustled myself down the stairs. I was hot under the collar, man. That Collins, I thought, sneaking in here to shoot hoops. All the while pretending to be up front at his post and making a stooge out of me on the walkie-talkie.

In the stairwell, that odor assaulted me. The stench wanted to suffocate me on the spot. I covered my nose and mouth with my hanky and bounced out to the basketball court.

There he was dangling right in front of my face. A young man hanging on a noose, swinging from the basketball net. Well, my knees buckled right out from under me, as if someone had slammed a two by four against them. I guess I passed out, cuz the next thing I knew, I was flat on my back, splayed out on the court. My head felt like one of Santa's elves was hammering it from the inside.

Real gingerly, I propped myself up. Man, that room was spinning. My head felt like it weighed a ton. I turned to look again at the hanged man, but he was gone. Not a trace of him left. That stink was gone, too.

I called Jesse the next day to see when he was coming back to work. We talked a bit.

"Go into the boys' gym?" Jesse asked.

"Sure," I said, real cautious.

"See anything weird?"

"Nah."

"Smell anything rancid?"

"'Course I did. It's a *boys' gym!*"

"Somebody's always bustin' my chops," Jesse whined.

Now, like I said earlier, I've seen a lot in my years at Giant. I've seen plenty of faces come and go. Heard plenty of wild stories too. One stuck with me. Back in 1968, before I ever came to Giant, a senior named Randy Stiles was riding a winning streak. Assured a full-ride basketball scholarship in the fall, he was basking in the glow of community fame.

He had a real pretty girlfriend named Jodi, and she planned to attend the same college. So things looked real sunny for Randy.

Randy's Achilles heel was his impulsiveness. *Tempestuous* is a nice writerly word you could use to describe him. Well, as fate would have it, one night after practice during that exceptional winning season, Jodi met him in the boys' gym. She broke things off right then and there. Without one peep of explanation, to boot.

Poor Randy, unaccustomed to defeat, succumbed to his first heartbreak. The next day, he hanged himself in his closet at home. That's where the story ends when most folks tell it. I think the tale continues a bit. I say that Randy's compelled to visit the boys' gym at Giant H.S., the site of his greatest victories and his most devastating defeat.

I don't know why I never told Jesse about what happened to me in the boys' gym that night. Never told Collins either. I never told anyone, not even my wife, until I wrote it all down here.

I don't go into the boys' gym
without my spleen somersaulting and
my eyes glued to that basketball net.
Far as I can tell, that hanging ghost
of Randy Stiles hasn't made another
appearance in 35 years.

But then again, I work days.

Flip Kuhlman
2006

Stormy Serena

In scouting for ghostly occurrences, I heard many people share tales of haunted cemeteries. Zosia Mucha's graveyard tale has remained with me. Rattled to the core by her experiences, Zosia swore me to secrecy and made me promise not to use her real name. She agreed to tell me the full story, without disclosing the precise location of the cemetery. However, she did admit that it was on a country road somewhere near Batavia, Illinois.

Batavia's history inspires awe. The Fabyan Windmill, constructed by a German craftsman in 1860 and still operational, stands sentinel over Route 25. Nearby is a spacious, vacant cage. Today, it's a popular spot for picnickers. However, it once housed two bears, Tom and Jerry, which occupied Colonel George Fabyan's private zoo.

In town, on Jefferson Street, rests Bellevue Place. Now a privately owned apartment building, it was once the private and rather luxurious sanitarium to which Mary Todd Lincoln was committed in 1875. So much unique history almost guarantees that there's a quirky ghost or two tromping around the town.

Zosia Mucha's personal history is quietly remarkable. A cruel influenza epidemic wiped out her entire family in Poland. In the 1980's, when they were in their twenties, Zosia and her husband Nikolai emigrated to the United States.

Side by side, they managed a successful country bakery. They were never blessed with children. Yet, Zosia and Nikolai were two peas in a pod, the best of friends. They created a thriving life in their adopted nation and enjoyed a loving marriage.

Since Nikolai's untimely death last spring, Zosia has become a bit weary, a touch melancholy. Now, as faithfully as she loved her husband, she tends his grave.

"Love never dies," Zosia told me the morning I visited her fragrant bakeshop. "I feel Nikolai's presence always. As often as I can, I visit his grave. I sit with him, talk to him—I share the day's little happenings. You might think me silly, but I bring Nikolai his favorite pastries."

"Not at all," I smiled.

One Sunday afternoon, Zosia placed fresh flowers on Nikolai's grave. It was a glorious day, sunny, not a cloud in the sky. Without warning, the heavens darkened. Howling winds swept over the cemetery. Lighting split the sky, and thunder cracked. As rain poured, Zosia dashed to a stone grotto for shelter.

"Looking out from the grotto," Zosia recalled, "I saw a young lady standing a short distance away. Ah, she was lovely! She had long black hair –almost to here." Zosia touched her waist.

"Her skin was creamy white and her lips were pale pink. Her dark hair rested on an ivory Edwardian dress. It was linen, finely embroidered and very old-fashioned. It made me think of the intricate needlework my *babcia* did in Poland."

"Did this woman rush into the grotto to take shelter with you?" I wondered.

"No, no," said Zosia. "It was so bizarre. She just stood right in the middle of the storm. The rain pelted her. The thunder continued to crash; truly, it was the loudest rumbling I've ever heard. It rocked the ground beneath my feet.

"As I watched, the young woman lifted a violin, tucked it neatly under her chin, and began to play. I recognized the piece instantly—Beethoven's *Moonlight Sonata.*"

As Zosia watched, the violinist abandoned herself to the music. Eyes closed, she swayed. She paid no attention to the raucous storm. In fact, Zosia explained, as the downpour progressed, the young woman played more furiously, thrashing dramatically and flailing her long hair.

"I thought she was someone like me, someone who had lost her love. Perhaps *Moonlight Sonata* was a special song for the violinist and her sweetheart.... I don't know.... I *do* know that there were moments when the thunder was so earsplitting that I couldn't hear the violin," Zosia said. "But whenever the thunder stilled itself, I heard that melancholy music drifting toward me."

As the storm subsided, the young woman stopped playing. She looked directly at Zosia, who waved her over to the grotto.

"I wanted to tell her how much I enjoyed her music. She walked slowly toward me," Zosia said. "As she got closer, I got a better look. Her clothes, her long hair—they were completely dry. And there was not a speck of rain on her ivory dress. My own hair was damp, clinging to my neck. My clothes and shoes were muddy from my sprint to the grotto. In contrast, the violinist was absolutely pristine."

As the young lady drew closer still, she smiled warmly at Zosia. To her astonishment, Zosia observed that the woman seemed to drift atop a swirling blue mist. Suddenly, the sun came out.

"Then—poof! The violinist vanished as if by a magician's hand," said Zosia.

Startled, Zosia hastened from the grotto and looked in all directions. The cemetery was silent.

Walking back to Nicholai's grave, Zosia passed a tombstone she had never noticed before.

"Serena Salmon," it read. "1898-1918." On the stone was an old black and white photo of the raven-haired Serena. Dressed in ivory, she proudly posed with her violin."

"It was the young lady who had serenaded me with the beautiful music," said Zosia. "This I know. I am *certain*." Emphatically, she pounded the counter where she was leaning.

I had absolutely no doubt of Zosia's sincerity. I asked, "Have you ever encountered her in the cemetery again?"

Zosia shook her head. "No, no, but I couldn't get her out of my mind. I still can't, if you want to know the truth. Yet, I didn't want to tell anyone. It's such a strange story; it defies reality. Nikolai's death has been so hard on me, and I didn't want to seem…"

I nodded sympathetically and gave her hand a quick squeeze.

"Eventually," Zosia continued, "My curiosity overwhelmed me, and I researched old newspapers at the library. I discovered that Serena Salmon died while playing her violin at a picnic. She was struck by lightning when a sudden squall blew in."

I guess the kind of storm Zosia experienced in the graveyard—one loud enough to wake the dead—kept Serena from resting in peace that Sunday afternoon.

A Bond That Will Last Forever

Nick Longo clapped his buddy Mitchell Bellini on the back, as the two met for their annual march in Wheaton's Memorial Day parade.

"Hey, *paisan*, where's your uniform?" Mitchell teased. He gave his old pal a friendly poke on the shoulder.

Nick shot back, "I can't even squeeze my pinky finger into that thing anymore. Were we ever really that skinny, Mitch?"

"Were we ever really that young?" Mitchell asked. Meticulously decked out in his dress uniform, he adjusted his cap and tilted it at a jaunty angle.

"Look at you, buddy boy," Nick marveled. "Not a hair out of place, not an ounce of fat on you, and not a moth bite besmirching your uniform. You're a credit to the Field Artillery Battalion, all right! How on God's green earth do you do it?"

"Just good, clean livin' for this GI," Mitchell said. "But I'll tell you what—this bum foot of mine sure the heck aches on chilly days like this. Be right back." He plopped on a bench, bent to remove his boot, and massaged the throbbing foot.

"World War II vets, line up right here, please," called a fresh-faced young woman who held a clipboard. She smiled at Nick.

"Good morning, Miss. I'm Nick, Nick Longo, hometown boy."

"I'm Tamara Collins from the city council. So nice to meet you, Mr. Longo." She shook his hand warmly.

"Shucks, call me Nick—I don't stand on ceremony. We're marching today in memory of our battalion buddies who can't be with us—for whatever reasons."

"We're delighted to have you, Nick."

"My friend Mitchell Bellini and I fought in General Patton's Third Army together. We forged a bond that will last forever. Forever. Mitch and I don't get to see each other as often as we'd like these days, but by jiminy, we make darned sure to get together every year for this parade."

Early in 1944, Nick and Mitchell met as teenagers in a winding enlistment line. At the time, Nick lived with his sizeable, raucous family in a cramped Wheaton apartment, while Mitchell hailed from a dairy farm. They had never once set a foot outside of Illinois. By the end of the year, the young comrades had toured more of Europe than they ever anticipated. Most times, Nick and Mitchell were side by side, shouldering as one the weary burden of battle.

In July, commanded by "Old Blood and Guts" Patton, Nick and Mitchell barreled through the German front near Cherbourg, France. In August, they assisted in the liberation of Paris. As the most frigid December anyone could recollect swept across Europe, they faced the gruesome Battle of the Bulge in Belgium. It proved the war's bloodiest battle.

Dead on their feet, sleep deprived, and lacking food, they endured the most harrowing days of their lives. Nick and Mitchell, realists both, hadn't expected to survive. They were ceaselessly astonished when they did.

In January of 1945, the devoted friends were separated—for the first time and for the remainder of the war. Mitchell was felled by trench foot, which eventually became gangrenous, and entered the hospital for treatment. Nick and Mitchell bid each other a temporary farewell.

"Doesn't it just figure that this bum foot would waylay me, after this crazy baptism by fire we've managed to live through?" Mitchell asked ruefully as he peeled open a K-Ration chocolate bar. "Promise you'll meet me back home—promise me. We'll marry sisters, have a million kids, live next door to each other in Wheaton—promise me."

"I promise," Nick said. "Godspeed." He wondered what the devil he would do without Mitchell at his side.

In April of 1945, Nick marched on with the Third Army to liberate the death camp at Buchenwald, Germany. The malevolent stench was permanently blazed in his nostrils. It was the stench of rotting corpses, despair, inhumanity. The hideous evidence of the atrocities Nick saw in the camp, which was littered with bodies stacked like cordwood, guaranteed that he never slept through the night for the rest of his life. Battle weary, he finally returned home and married Doris, a girl he met in his new job at the post office. Nick told her about the death camps, once. Then, he took a private vow of silence. He never spoke of them again.

Yet, he often woke up screaming and covered in perspiration with the bedclothes tangled around his body and Doris sitting bolt upright in terror beside him. Thankfully, Nick had Mitchell with whom to discuss the ghosts of the past, battlefield and otherwise. The two friends didn't have to talk, really, they just *understood*.

Nick vowed to embrace each day as a gift, and he saw to it that his two sons and wife received all the love he had to offer. He proudly displayed the United States flag on the Wheaton bungalow he and Doris bought in 1950, and he insisted that his sons be named in honor of fallen comrades.

Now, Nick's sons were grown and living out of state, with kids of their own. Nick socialized at the VFW hall and never missed a Friday fish fry. He never missed the Memorial Day parade, either. It was his yearly opportunity to spend time with Mitchell, march once more as comrades, side by side, and reminisce about old times.

"How would you like to toss candy to the kids in the crowd, Nick?" asked Tamara.

"You don't have to ask me twice, though my aim's a little rusty," Nick said. He took a bag of sweets from Tamara and lined up beside Mitchell, who was shifting his weight to ease his aching foot. "Ready, Mitchell?"

"Hey, you don't mind if I lean on you a bit, do you?" Mitchell grimaced. "This blasted foot's gonna be the death of me, I swear."

By the parade's conclusion, Mitchell was noticeably limping, and Nick's knees were popping like firecrackers. Nick spotted Tamara waving to them and hustled over to her. A child stood beside her.

"Nick, I'd like you to meet my son, Justin," she said. "Justin, this is Mr. Longo."

"Hey there, Justin." Nick tipped his cap. "Now, Tamara and Justin, I'd like you to meet my best buddy ever, Mitchell Bellini. Mitch and I were in the Field Artillery Battalion together, and he saved my sorry behind on more than one occasion—excuse my French."

Puzzled, Tamara peered at Nick, who stood alone. He gestured expansively to the vacant space beside him.

"You must be tired, Nick, can I get you some cold water?" she asked gently.

"Mommy! Look at the candy the man gave me," cried Justin. He opened his palm gleefully.

"Justin, what—what man? Where on earth did that old thing come from?" cried Tamara.

"That nice man with Mr. Longo. That man with the sore foot. He gave it to me."

Flashing his toothless grin, Justin clutched a K-Ration chocolate bar.

Another Cup for Willa

"Let me just tell you right off the bat that I didn't believe in ghosts. To me, it was a whole lot of hooey. But I changed my mind when Willa started visiting me."

Cheryl Ann chomped off the end of her slim cigar and spit it into the air with a jubilant, "Patooie!" She lit up, took more than a few puffs, and blasted the smoke out of her mouth in a trail of O's.

"Got me?" She squinted, searching my face.

"Gotcha," I replied. I fanned the smoke away from my face with my notepad.

Cheryl Ann and I sat in shabby chic wicker chairs on the front porch of her old home in the historic part of Geneva. No two houses are alike in Cheryl Ann's neighborhood, which oozes character and bygone days. A short walk from Geneva's scenic downtown, her cottage is meticulously restored and lovingly maintained, like many others in the picturesque town. Cheryl Ann, a descendant of the Swedish immigrants that settled in Geneva in the 1890's, is enormously proud of her ties to the community.

Max, Cheryl Ann's placid chocolate Lab, nestled at my feet. Periodically, he rose to snatch a pinecone from the ground and trot hopefully my way. A sucker for a furry face, I hurled the cone for him to retrieve.

"In fact," Cheryl Ann continued in her cantankerous way, "I take issue with your using the word *ghost*. I prefer *spirit*. *Ghost* sounds creepy and sinister. Willa's spirit is loving and playful."

I've known Cheryl Ann for years. A no-nonsense high school history teacher, she impatiently suffers fools and has a temper as red-hot as her hair. She pulls no punches and shoots from the hip, so you always know exactly where you stand with her. She reminds me of a feisty, hard-boiled dame from an old film noir. Yet, she's the kind of friend who will toast your victories and haul you uphill when you've hit rock bottom. I adore her.

"Nothing prepares you for losing your best friend—nothing," Cheryl Ann explained. "Willa was diagnosed with leukemia on May 12 in 2005. A year later she was gone. She never even made it to her fortieth birthday, which makes me outrageously angry."

Ever the pugilist, Cheryl Ann stomped the creaky porch beneath our feet.

"Initially, I acted like a raving lunatic when Willa died. I was impossible to deal with, I kid you not."

I had no doubt, but I held my tongue.

Cheryl Ann went on. "I was accustomed to taking my tribulations to Willa, so I didn't know what to do with them in her absence. And of course, all my troubles revolved around losing her. Yeah, for a while there, I was as out of control as a dust devil on Mars.

"Willa and I used to meet here every Saturday morning. We'd stroll all the way to Mount St. Mary's Park in St. Charles. It was one of our favorite haunts. We'd jabber furiously, yak about our jobs, the troubles of the world, you name it. Then, we'd come back here and brew up a pot of cinnamon tea, Willa's favorite.

"The day Willa told me that she was sick, it felt like someone karate-chopped me in the throat. I couldn't breathe. Hey, here's her picture."

Cheryl Ann reached into her pocket, withdrew a photo, and passed it to me. I studied it. Doe-eyed Willa looked thoughtfully back at me from behind funky red glasses. She seemed to be gazing directly into my eyes.

"The worst part of the whole thing was that Willa didn't want any visitors during her final days. She was such a proud woman—vain, really. She didn't want her friends to remember her the way she was in the hospice. I'm still grappling with that. I wish Willa hadn't shut me out."

Cheryl Ann tilted her head back, gnawed on her cigar, and considered the towering blue spruce in her yard.

"I can't change that now," Cheryl Ann sighed. "I'm furious at Willa over it. But it was her call, so I need to come to grips with it, don't I?

"Now, bit by bit by bit, Willa's been easing my anger. She makes her presence known, pops in to check on me. Never says a word, though. Hey, did I tell you that Willa manipulates electricity?"

"She *what?*" I asked.

"Fiddles around with electricity. Does it all the time—flickers the lights, turns the TV on and off, makes my alarm clock go off at odd hours."

"When did she come to see you the first time?" I asked and tossed a pinecone for mellow Max.

"That was just last month, on my birthday, July 20. Willa and I always did the same thing for our birthdays—we went kayaking along the Fox. On my birthday, I faced the death of that tradition.

It was a lousy day for me. Probably the worst in my whole life. I was home all by my lonesome. Had the comforter pulled over my head like it was the dead of winter. I felt so frozen inside, it might as well have *been* winter.

"I was about to twitch right out of my skin. Just didn't know what to do with myself. Suddenly, the doorbell rang. Well, I forced myself to crawl out of bed. I opened the front door, but no one was there. At first I blamed those little ruffians next door, bless their hearts. Ding Dong Ditch never goes out of style, my friend.

"I went back inside, put on a kettle for tea, and set out my favorite Spode cup—the one with the teensy little periwinkle flowers. Well, the doorbell rang again. The same thing happened when I went to answer it. Wasn't a soul there. I stepped outside and peeked this way and that way down the block."

Cheryl Ann gestured toward the Victorian farmhouse to our right and the Frank Lloyd Wright at our left. As I said, she lives in the historic part of Geneva.

"Well, by then my kettle was whistling like crazy. I trotted myself back into the kitchen. You won't believe this."

With warm fingers, Cheryl Ann seized my arm. I held my breath.

"There were two cups waiting on the counter—two. And there was a cinnamon teabag in one of them."

I felt my scalp tingle. Goosebumps rose on my arms.

"Ready for the weirdest part?" Cheryl Ann continued. "Just then, while I was still attempting to hoist my dropped jaw off the floor, the blasted bell rang. I heaved that door open and shot out to the porch. I was determined to catch my merry prankster. Once again, the porch was as empty as a beer keg after a frat party. But I got a good, healthy whiff of lavender, Willa's signature scent. I can almost smell in now, thinking about her. Can you?" Cheryl Ann inhaled deeply.

"Sorry, all I smell is that stinky cigar." I laughed, but I have to admit, I was growing a bit uneasy.

"Let's go in and brew up a pot of cinnamon tea. We'll drink to Willa," suggested Cheryl Ann, as she stubbed out her cigar. "I might be tempted to open a nice, fruit-forward cabernet, too."

Inside Cheryl Ann's narrow kitchen
we waited for the kettle to whistle.
Abruptly, Max began madly barking,
and an instant later we heard, *Ding,
dong!*

"I'll get it," I told Cheryl Ann and
took a few strides to the door. I
opened it inquisitively, with a smile.
Geneva's a neighborly place.

The front porch was vacant. The
strong scent of soothing lavender
wafted over me.

I couldn't locate my voice. Mouth
agape, I whirled around. Cheryl Ann
hovered directly behind me.

"Let me grab another cup for Willa," Cheryl Ann called,
heading back to the kitchen.

"She's dropping in at one of her favorite haunts."

River's Edge

Becca Marcotte, aged 10, of St. Charles was utterly convinced that her mother, endlessly expecting, could control the sex of the children she bore. Thus, Becca proved endlessly exasperated when Liam, her sixth younger brother, joined the family.

"No, Mom, not again," she moaned. "Not *another brother.*"

Grudgingly, Becca had to admit that there was something endearing about the way Liam grasped her finger in his tiny fist. The way he gazed at her with unquestioned trust. The way he was so different from the rest. While her other brothers smelled of musty earth and worms, Liam wore the scent of a cool breeze.

In time, Becca allowed little Liam to capture her heart. No longer exasperated, she became endlessly protective.

By the time Liam was three, Becca joked that her middle name was Keep an Eye on Your Brothers. At any given moment, there was a ragtag assortment of brothers, their companions, and their various critters—furred, finned, and feathered—to look after.

"Trying to corral the Brothers Marcotte," Becca grumbled, "is like herding cats in a sandstorm."

The five other Brothers Marcotte were a whooping, hollering handful. They sprinted across streets without looking and hid snakes under Becca's bed. They popped out of the clothes hamper to revel in her screams of terror. Once, the gleeful cabal even leapt from the garage roof for the sheer pleasure of watching the color drain from Becca's face.

Mostly, Becca kept her eyes on Liam. Not as rambunctious as the others, Liam rarely strayed too far, though occasionally, he squirmed from her grasp. Fortunately, Becca's arms were so long and her reflexes—honed as they were by the unruly Brothers Marcotte—so speedy that she easily pulled him close when the urge to flee overtook him.

Liam was born with a lazy eye. The ophthalmologist prescribed an eye patch to train the eye into taking further responsibility for Liam's sight. With the black patch over his eye and his vivid imagination in action, Liam pretended he was a pirate. However, with his stronger eye covered, he often misjudged distances when galloping upstairs, leaping into bed, or even walking at a leisurely pace.

All the more reason, Becca knew, to keep a good grip on her youngest brother.

Walking along the riverfront near Pottawatomie Pavilion that July day in 1993, Becca clutched the back of Liam's shirt collar.

"Stay close, Matey," Becca said.

Freed after being trapped indoors for several days of severe weather, Liam was delighted by their surroundings. He gawked at the swollen river, the result of torrential rains that summer. Broken branches, knobby refugees of the previous night's fierce winds, zipped across the river as if motored.

"Look, look," he squealed, gesturing to a fallen branch sailing their way. Perched in a bumpy crook, a turtle lazed in the sun. "The turtle's a pirate, too."

Becca spun around to watch the tiny buccaneer's voyage. In that quick motion, she momentarily released Liam's collar. Like a terrier in pursuit of a rabbit, he darted away and scampered down the mossy shoreline. When he leaned forward for a closer peek at the armored sailor, he cartwheeled over the slickness.

In slow motion, Becca watched as Liam toppled headfirst over the river wall. The high-velocity waters swallowed him in a single greedy gulp. Somewhere far, far in the back of her mind, she wondered, "Who is making that awful noise?"

Too terrified to recognize the sound of her own screams, Becca bolted to the slippery shoreline. One leg slid crazily out from the other. She felt the searing pain of her torn muscle, willed herself to rise, and searched frantically for Liam.

Truth be told, if someone had seized her at that very instant and asked her which horrified her more, knowing that the river had kidnapped Liam or knowing that she would be held responsible, Becca would have been stumped.

Flailing her arms and shrieking until her throat was raw, Becca hobbled beneath the willows that lined the shore. She fought back the urge to vomit as she limped toward the bridge. In an instant, she would reach the riverfront police station, where she could yell for help.

"Please, oh, please, oh, please." She prayed aloud. "Please let him be—"

Miraculously, she saw him.

Liam, drenched but composed, was perched on a flat rock on the shore. She hurled herself at him, scooped him into her arms, and sobbed. Her breath was ragged, the pain in her leg forgotten

"How did you get here?" she asked finally. She wiped away the tears that trailed down her cheeks, leaving muddy streaks across her face.

"He gave me a ride in his canoe," Liam said.

"Who did? What canoe?" Boats were prohibited because of the high waters.

"The Indian man. Like the statue." Liam flapped his chubby arm toward a sculpture at the river's edge. Depicting a member of the mighty Potawatomi nation, original settlers of the Fox Valley, the bronze monument provided a lookout above the bloated river.

"Gosh, Liam," Becca chuckled, despite herself. "That's some imagination you have."

Liam bunched the end of his shirt and twisted it like a sopping towel, spattering water over Becca's feet.

"Shiver me timbers, Matey!" Becca said. "We better get home before you catch your death of cold. Mom and Dad are going to wring my neck for bringing you here. I'll be grounded for the rest of my natural days."

"'K," said Liam. He adjusted his eye patch, slipped his damp hand into Becca's, and took a few steps. Then he stopped.

Turning back, he waved to the river—or someone in it. Then, with the loving weight of Becca's hand on the back of his neck, he set off for home.

"The spirits of my ancestors have never left this great Valley...."

Inscription on the statue titled *Ekwabet,*
which means "watching over." The
statue stands alongside the Fox River in
St. Charles' Pottawatomie Park.

The Phantom Panthers

Wilbur Hawkings of Wayne put me in contact with a friend of his, Bud McMasters, who works as a farm hand in Algonquin. A Texas transplant, Bud claimed that a ramshackle cabin located on the property of the farm was haunted.

"You that writer lady Wilbur told me 'bout?" Bud greeted me with a lopsided grin. "Not one o' them yuppified cappuccino-breath ladies, are ya?"

I laughed. "Wilbur tells me you've experienced an eerie encounter," I began.

"Heck, yes!" Bud said. "Ya'd think it would be more appropriate for a punkin farm to be crawlin' with haints. But no, this ol' dairy farm's got phantom panthers traipsin' 'round and causin' a general ruckus. I ran into 'em up at the shack one night. Lemme tell ya all about it."

"Please do," I said. I was fully aware that panthers are extinct in Illinois. However, that was evidently a quibbling point that didn't appear to trouble the phantoms Bud happened upon.

Bud said, "I ain't never gonna forget that night. It was darker'n midnight under a skillet. Me 'n' my beagle Bertha were near the shack, which is way off in the back forty. I was holdin' my lantern. Bertha was scoutin' a raccoon that was givin' us thirteen kinds of grief. Well, no sooner had Bertha treed that coon, when a gullywasher swept in.

"That storm was a real frog strangler, I'll tell ya. Bertha 'n' me, we lit out like coyotes was after us. Ran right inside the shack. Now, that ol' shack is hangin' together with spit 'n' a prayer. Looks like you could blow it over easy as whooshin' out a candle on a birthday cake. I wasn't too wild 'bout takin' shelter there. But I had no choice."

"I can certainly understand that," I said.

Bud went on, "Once we jumped inside, I shined my lantern from stem to stern. I got me a real surprise."

He leaned closer, speaking in a hushed voice.

"Ya see, there were chunks of wood all nice and neat in the fireplace. Was a fancy set of andirons there, too. Shaped just like cattails. Now, far as I knew up 'til then, nobody used that decrepit ol' shack. I figured maybe me 'n' Bertha was intrudin' on a romantic interlude or somethin'."

Bud snickered.

"Well, ma'am, I lit that fire fast as I could. I was happier than a gopher in soft dirt to find the wood waitin' for me, after all."

Bud and Bertha settled on the musty dirt floor to wait for the storm to pass. Bud perspired in anxiety. The fear that the squall would wreck havoc on the flimsy shack gnawed at him.

"All of a sudden," Bud continued, "the door burst open. Ol' Bertha started bayin' for dear life. A big ol' panther crept inside, just as sassy as you please. That cat slammed the door behind him 'n' set smack-dad in the middle of the roaring fire like it was a hot bath."

The black panther, Bud explained, had a long, broad tail. Its body appeared to be about four feet long. With yellowish-green eyes that glowed like coals, it studied Bud, who squirmed under its scrutiny.

"He licked his chops 'n' eyed me 'n' Bertha like we was a tasty platter of chicken-fried steak."

The panther threw back its glossy head and roared. Leisurely swishing its tail, it purred.

"Just you wait until Levi gets here," the panther said.

Bud pinched himself once, twice.

"I couldn't believe my ears."

Then, the panther sprawled beside Bud, who tried to ignore the ebony interloper.

"Well, Bertha was whinin' 'n' wigglin' 'n' chompin' at the bit to give chase, but I grasped her real tight."

A few moments passed. To petrified Bud, it seemed like an era. The door blew open again and a second panther sauntered in.

Bud said, "Now, this second cat was even bigger—'bout six feet long. He stomped inside, ambled over to the fireplace, 'n' fetched himself an andiron. First, he scratched his back with it. Then, just as deliberate as you please, he sharpened his claws on the metal. Never took his eyes off us neither."

Holding Bertha for dear life, Bud trembled. He listened, bug-eyed as the second panther nudged the first.

"What are we going to do with them?"

Then, explained Bud, "That second panther eyeballed me 'n' Bertha, real greedy-like. I tell ya, that ravenous cat made a hornet look cuddly!"

The first panther roared, flashing fangs like ochre daggers.

"We are going to do nothing, nothing at all, until Levi gets here," it said.

The second panther slowly circled Bud and Bertha. After an excruciatingly long time, the second panther licked its drooling chops and settled next to the first.

"Well, by now," Bud continued, "I was scared out o' of my wits. I took one look at the claws on that second beast 'n' I knew he could swipe my head clean off."

Bud's mind clicked a mile a minute as he desperately plotted an escape attempt. Just then, the door blasted open a third time.

"Now, that door busted open so hard that it splintered. It twisted all cattywhompus on the hinges. An enormous panther jest sashayed inside. I tell you what. That ol' cat was big as a pick-up truck, 'n' he was about as appreciated as a buzzard at a lawn party. He tromped himself right over to the fire. Sifted through the flames. Grabbed the heaviest log 'n' picked his ol' fangs with it like it was a toothpick. Then he snatched up the other andiron 'n' whet his teeth on it."

At length, the third panther gracefully bounded across the shack. Its ferocious snarl rattled the walls, and the ground rocked beneath its massive body. As the third panther lounged beside the others, Bud tried not to gawk at its brawny chest, its fearsome claws, and its mighty jaws, which could crush his skull like an eggshell.

"In a heartbeat that terrible trio would be all over us like stink on skunk," said Bud. "Then that third panther spoke with a rumbling voice that made my toes curl."

"What are we going to do with them?"

The other panthers growled. Their sulfur eyes glowed.

"We are going to do nothing, nothing at all, until Levi gets here."

Bud scrambled to his feet and grasped wriggling Bertha beneath his arm.

"I sure do appreciate your hospitality, fellers," he announced. "But I jest got to fly. Give my regards to ol' Levi when he finally moseys on over here."

And with that, Bud and Bertha high-tailed it out into the stormy night.

Someone's Pride and Joy

"Jas, you won't believe what I found in that old shed," said Aziz.

Her hair tucked inside a baseball cap, Jasmine stood on a stepladder. She painstakingly painted the front door of the Greek Revival cottage in Carpentersville, several miles from the Fox River Trail bike path.

The door, set at the right corner of the house, was the original. Almost 175 years old, as Aziz was fond of pointing out. When Jasmine first laid eyes on it, she knew she had found the home of her dreams. An off-center door, she claimed, was a tribute to an independent spirit.

Painting the door was one of the final jobs to be tackled during their yearlong restoration of the cottage. Jasmine, with her steady hand and her eye for detail, insisted on doing the honors, while Aziz cleared out the rickety shed at the far corner of the yard.

"I'm paining the door bright red, to symbolize our passion for the house," Jasmine declared.

Next to the door was a placard on which was carved "1833," the home's date of completion. Beneath the low-pitched gable roof with its broad cornice return was a fine dentil moulding, which Aziz recovered it from a salvage shop in Chicago and labored to apply. A perfect period addition, as Jasmine was fond of pointing out.

"What did you find?" Jasmine asked, still intent on her painting.

"A rusty old scythe, a couple of awls that have seen better days, and the *pièce de résistance*, an antique sled. A kid's sled, I think."

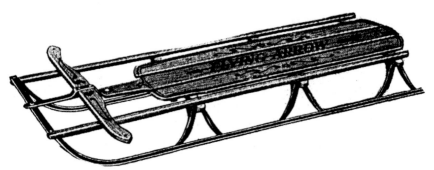

Jasmine stepped down from the ladder and crouched to admire the hickory sled. Its partial bentwood rise was decorated with iron swan's head finials. Runners, with sturdy iron strips reinforcing the honey-colored wood, flawlessly curved inward from the rise.

"How cool is that?" asked Aziz.

"It's spectacular," said Jasmine. "Once upon a time, this sled was someone's pride and joy."

Aziz said, "It's pretty worn—"

"Well loved."

"—But look at the craftsmanship.
Let's clean this baby and polish it up.
Renovate and rejuvenate it, like
we've done with the house."

"We'll give it a good home,"
Jasmine agreed. "You know, it
would make a fabulous table to tuck
in a nook somewhere."

"Sure you don't want to sell it to an
antique dealer? We could probably
get a pretty penny for it."

"No, it's staying with the house. It
fits right in."

Although Jasmine crashed into bed that night, her sleep was
restless. She had never felt more fatigued or more exhilarated in
her life, a combination that resulted in a body too drained to
battle an active mind. The utter exhaustion she felt after a year
of living among torn-down walls and lifted floorboards, of
dodging tarps and strategically placing buckets to catch rain
water was tempered by her exquisite pleasure in a goal attained.

She woke repeatedly, dwelled on odds and ends that required her attention, wondered where to place the sled.

"I can't turn my brain off," she thought. "It's relentless."

After hours of tossing and turning, she finally fell into a reasonably deep sleep.

The soft weeping awoke her.

Jasmine sat upright, reaching breathlessly for her glasses and slipping them on. Quite distinctly, she saw the outline of a slight figure at the foot of the bed.

The weeping increased, became a plaintive wail, and reached a chilling crescendo. The figure, a young girl who was wringing her hands, glided toward Jasmine.

"She looks like a porcelain doll," Jasmine marveled.

Clearly, Jasmine saw the girl's blonde ringlets bobbing as she sobbed. She noticed the child's calico dress, with its lace Bertha collar, and her pantalettes demurely peeking from the hem.

Inexplicably, Jasmine addressed the child by name.

"Abigail, why are you crying?"

"My sled," Abigail sobbed, as she hovered, illuminated, above the bed. "My sled. I want my sled." She rose toward the ceiling, where she lingered like a wispy cloud.

A slim ray of sunlight slid through a crack in the curtain and zigzagged across Jasmine's eyes. She heard Aziz puttering in the kitchen and rose from bed.

"What an eerie dream," she thought. "I can still hear Abigail's weeping."

She slid into her dressing gown and hurried to the kitchen. Aziz, studying the sled with wariness, scrubbed it with a damp cloth.

"Oh, hi, I didn't hear you get up. Jas, I had the freakiest dream about a little girl last night—like a vision," he said. "I'm putting the sled back in the shed, where it belongs."

Solemnly, Jasmine nodded. "Abigail came to me too. We've disrupted her terribly, Aziz, with our renovation."

"Let me finish polishing the sled. My dad always said, 'When you borrow something, make it a little better before you give it back.'"

"Good," said Jasmine. "That sled is Abigail's pride and joy."

Aziz returned the scythe and awls, along with the sled, to the shed where he had found them. He built a placard, "Abigail's House," and stuck it into the ground next to the shed.

After that, Aziz and Jasmine left the old shed untouched. As far as one call tell, their actions pleased Abigail. She never made another appearance in the house, although on snowy days, Aziz and Jasmine have found sled tracks circling the shed.

In the Attic

Eulalia Buckthorn, married merely one year and pushed to her capacity, fled to her parents' home in Aurora. There, she whispered terrible secrets about her brutal husband, Edward.

"You will return to your husband. You will beg his forgiveness," her stern father Samuel commanded. "The shame of divorce will not darken our doorstep."

"But Father, you haven't listened to me," said Eulalia.

"Your ingratitude appalls me, for I chose your husband with the utmost consideration. Edward is a Civil War hero. He trained with General Farnsworth at Camp Kane and distinguished himself at Gettysburg. You will not disrespect Edward with your capricious ways."

"Father, I cannot endure one more day with that dreadful—"

"You will not disobey my wishes. Come, follow me."

79

Samuel escorted Eulalia to his carriage. He personally delivered her to Edward's home in Oswego, the town at the confluence of the Fox River and Waubonsie Creek.

Edward offered thanks in his oily fashion. He wrapped his burly arm around Eulalia's corseted waist and murmured something about a lover's spat. Serenely, he shook hands with his father-in-law. Then, side by side, Edward and Eulala waved farewell as Samuel climbed into his carriage.

The minute the carriage was out of view, Edward led Eulalia inside their narrow three-story home. His meaty paw at her back, Edward urged her up the stairs to the attic. He thrust her inside and slammed the door. He ignored first the whimpers, then the screams and panic-stricken pounding from within, the frenzied attempts at escape. He simply bolted the door and retreated victoriously to his study.

Folks scarcely saw Eulalia after that. After several months, Edward, head bowed in grief, informed the neighbors that Eulalia had run off with another man.

The shallow grave behind the house told another story.

Over the years, the home, abandoned and heirless, fell into disrepair. It offered its paltry hospitality to train tramps that passed a fleeting night or two under its leaky roof or to teenagers that crept inside to smoke. Yet, even the vagrants who sought shelter there didn't remain in the house long. They complained of thumping and wailing in the attic, of the sounds of someone pacing like a caged animal. A pair of squatters who attempted to take up residence in the house reportedly barreled out the front door in the middle of the night, panting and wide-eyed in fright.

It wasn't until 1950's, when the post-war baby boom was at its peak, that Cole Rachman, his wife Kathleen, and their infant daughter moved in. And it wasn't long after their arrival that Cole, a cold man with a hot temper and an unquenchable thirst for whiskey, drew the attention of the neighbors.

While Cole was at his job at the tractor plant, Kathleen asked a friend to sit with baby Dorothea for a few hours. Kathleen never returned. She and a traveling salesman from Chicago headed off for parts unknown. At least, that's what Cole confided to the inquisitive neighbors.

Unfit as Kathleen was to be a
mother, Cole sneered, she left
Dorothea behind—abandoned her.

It was an unfortunate situation to
be sure, the neighbors tsk-tsked.
Yet, they kept their distance from
Cole, with his glinty eyes and his
junkyard dog demeanor. Such a
shame for Dorothea, they clucked.
Poor dear, poor motherless lamb.
From a comfortable distance, they
watched Dorothea mature.

Season followed season.
Turbulent times in the world
mirrored turbulent times in the
Rachman home.

Cole Rachman practiced two methods of expression—silence
and rage. Dorothea, who possessed the vast misfortune of
looking exactly like her mother, was the recipient of both.
The more ornery Cole grew, the more Dorothea relied on her
fierce determination.

"I won't be like him. I won't," she swore. "I will escape to a
better life, like my mother did."

When Cole wasn't around to berate her for wasting time with
her nose buried in a book, she sought refuge on a weathered
bench beneath an ancient oak tree in the backyard. Immersed in
her reading, she lost all sense of time and place. Her favorite
book was *Joan of Arc,* a tattered volume she had discovered,
long forgotten, beneath an attic floorboard.

Head bent over her book, Dorothea could almost feel the light touch of a reassuring hand on her back.

Thankfully, Cole's old truck announced itself with sputters and clangs before making its sickly way uphill on the gravel driveway. The racket allowed Dorothea enough time to race indoors and bolt upstairs to her cramped attic room. There, safe from Cole's wrath, Dorothea could almost feel soothing fingers stroking her chestnut hair.

After years of enduring Cole's silences and rages, Dorothea fully opened herself to the latter. At 18, she announced her intention to attend college in the East.

"You can't go to college," Cole sneered. "Where do you think you're getting that kind of money?"

Calmly, Dorothea said, "I have a scholarship to study literature, Dad—"

"Literature, eh? As usual, putting on airs. Miss Highfalutin' Priss."

"—and I have just about every cent I've ever earned from my jobs."

"Think you're better than me, don't you? Slingin' hash just isn't good enough for Miss Priss, is it? You're just like *her*."

Dorothea's face burned. She imagined herself as Joan of Arc, stepping into the security of her chain mail and deflecting the torrent of malicious words Cole hurled at her.

She tried to be cavalier. Why should this response be any different?

The silence set in then—five months of uneasy stillness. Dorothea came and went in its chill, avoiding her father as best she could. Mornings, she remained in the attic until Cole departed for his job at the factory. After he drank himself to sleep in the evenings, she crept home from her job at the Granite Grill.

As her eagerly anticipated departure date approached, Dorothea packed her meager belongings in several boxes. On her desk calendar, she counted off the remaining days until her best friend's father would drive both girls off to college. To escape, to a new life.

At last, the day arrived. Arduously, she lugged her boxes down the narrow stairway from the attic, stooping under the low-slung ceiling. She nearly dropped her battered typewriter when Carl leapt out unsteadily from the kitchen.

"Where do you think you're going?" he roared.

"It's time, Dad," Dorothea said. She felt immensely sad. "I'm leaving for college with Maddy. Mr. Czech is driving us."

"Well, you're not taking any of this stuff." He kicked one of Dorothea's boxes peevishly.

"Please, Dad, don't. These are all my things. My books, my clothes, my photos. I paid for everything. It's all mine."

"You came to me with nothing. You'll leave that way."

Unsteady from the drink, Cole wobbled toward her, teeth bared.

Dorothea's boxes, neatly taped and labeled, levitated simultaneously. Surrounded by a luminous cloud, they drifted past Cole, out the door, and into the yard.

Cole scratched his stubbly chin in astonishment. He lunged at one of the boxes, missed, and tumbled against the bottom of the stairway.

"Go outside, dear Dorothea," a soft voice whispered. "Come, follow me."

An unseen arm gently embraced Dorothea's shoulder and escorted her to the door. Beneath her feet, Dorothea felt a strange surge of energy, an alien force that held her aloft and propelled her forward. She floated outside, watching the grass and the gravel driveway below her feet.

Gradually, the mysterious force relinquished its pressure. Dorothea's feet noiselessly coasted to the ground. She heard the crunch of gravel as Mr. Czech's car approached and saw Maddy, half her body extended from the passenger window, waving elatedly.

"Woo hoo!" Maddy yelled.

Breathless, Dorothea loaded her boxes into Mr. Czech's car. Maddy climbed into the back seat, and Dorothea followed.

"You're shaking like a leaf," Maddy said. "I'm excited too."

Dorothea smiled wanly. She never glanced back at the house, never saw the young woman in the long dress who dragged Cole up the stairs and shoved him into the attic. Precisely the way the young woman had shoved Cole years ago, when he caught Dorothea's mother packing her bags and attempted to hinder her escape.

Dorothea never heard Cole pounding the attic door, his brawny shoulder a frantic battering ram.

"College, here we come," cried Maddy. "Onward!"

Several days later, Dorothea unpacked in the dorm. She discovered among her possessions an unfamiliar tintype photograph in an ornate gilded frame. Its grainy image showed a bespectacled young woman with dark hair piled high. She wore a long dress with a full, ruffled skirt. At her throat was a dark ribbon. Head bent, she sat on a bench beneath an oak tree—Dorothea's bench.

The young woman was engrossed in a book, *Joan of Arc*.

The Gold Coin

Nancy Lee of McHenry endures grueling physical training each year as she prepares for the Chicago Marathon. McHenry's Moraine Hills State Park is one of her favorite places to train.

"The beauty of the surroundings," Nancy said, "provides a refreshing inspiration when I'm running. I drink in the wonders of nature and forget about the way I'm pummeling my body."

A moraine is an enormous amassing of earth, including soil, boulders, and other stone debris, which is carried and eventually deposited by a glacier. When glacial ice melted long, long ago, it created the lakes, marshes, and bogs that mark the region.

Today, Moraine Hills State Park is a wildlife enthusiast's delight. It's a haven for cross-country skiers, hikers, cyclists, and picnickers. All share the area with an array of inhabitants including minks, red foxes, beavers, white-tailed deer, and all manner of waterfowl.

Nancy Lee, whose ancestors date to the *Mayflower*, shared a story that had been handed down in her family through the oral tradition. The incident took place just after the Civil War, almost a century before Moraine Hills opened to the public. Nancy is uncertain of the precise location in which her tale is set; however, she does know that it is somewhere near the present-day state park.

Albert and Lavinia Montressor were honeymooning at a lovely and secluded inn located in McHenry. One brisk afternoon, they rented a carriage and set out to explore the autumn countryside.

The woods were hushed. The forest's musicians, orange orioles and golden-yellow warblers, had taken flight for warmer wintering places. Most of the trees were bare, stripped of the glorious fall colors that, only a week earlier, had adorned them. Here and there, lonesome stragglers bravely gripped bony branches. Damp clumps of leaves clung to a stony ridge where Albert and Lavinia stopped to take their ease.

Lavinia admired an old copper sundial atop the ridge. Tremendously tarnished, it was decorated with carved suns and moons. As she shined it with her glove, Lavinia felt fall's chilly fingers ruffle her curls. She quivered in the crisp air of the woods and snuggled deliciously into her velvet cloak.

Meanwhile, Albert located an immense tree stump beyond the ridge. Playfully sitting on it, he called Lavinia to join him. When she did, Lavinia rested her head against Albert's shoulder, and the weary travelers dozed.

In time the honeymooners awoke with a start. Darkness had settled, and it was nearly impossible to discern the rugged dirt road that led back to their inn.

"Oh, dear, Albert, whatever shall we do?" asked Lavinia.

"Don't fret, dearest," Albert replied. "I see a light glowing in the clearing. There must be a house. Perhaps we can pass the night with its owners."

Albert drove the carriage toward the cedar cottage. An elderly man and his wife stood in the arched doorway and brandished a lantern expectantly. The elderly couple invited the honeymooners inside and insisted that Albert and Lavinia join them for a simple supper of pea soup and crusty bread.

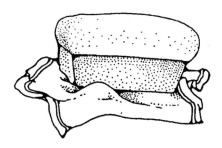

After the pleasant meal, the elderly couple showed Albert and Lavinia to a bedchamber. There, a welcoming fire roared, and freshly laundered linens covered the birch bed.

"You are so very kind," said Lavinia. "It's almost as if you were expecting us."

"Indeed, we are greatly appreciative of your hospitality," said Albert. "Please allow me to offer payment for—"

"Dear me, no," said the elderly woman. "We are simply opening our hearts and home to those who journey this way."

"We have vowed to welcome those who wander in the night," said her husband.

The couples, one just beginning their journey together and the other long companions on theirs, bid each other good night.

Albert and Lavinia arose at daybreak and departed quietly, so as not to disturb their hosts. Before they left, Albert removed a gold coin from his pocket and polished it with his handkerchief until it gleamed. He placed the coin on the table where supper had been served.

"I want them to know how grateful I am," Albert murmured. He had observed that the elderly twosome were of extremely modest means, and he wished to repay their generosity.

Albert and Lavinia returned to the lovely inn, where they shared with Carlotta the innkeeper their adventure of the previous night. The innkeeper's hand flew to her throat.

"*Where* was it that you spent the night?"

Albert and Lavinia described the stony ridge that bordered the home and the gigantic stump beyond it. Lavinia raved about the antique sundial.

"I do believe that you are confused," said Carlotta. "That home belonged to Amos and Margaret Finch. They were noted Abolitionists in this area who provided a station on the Underground Railroad. Amos and Margaret helped many escaped slaves follow the Drinking Gourd to freedom."

"Why do you say that we're confused?" wondered Albert.

"Tragically, Amos and Margaret died in the very house that offered sanctuary to others. A fire burned it to the ground years ago."

"I must say that *you* are the one who is confused," said Lavinia. "For we surely passed the night with the fine couple of whom you speak."

Arms akimbo, Carlotta stood firm.

"You are in error," she said.

Equally resolute, Lavinia cooed, "I beg to differ. We most certainly are not."

To settle the disagreement, Albert, Lavinia, and Carlotta set off in the carriage to locate the disputed home in the woods. At length, Lavinia noted the stony ridge, the copper sundial, and the enormous tree stump.

The trio left the carriage and made their way through the clearing. They came upon the charred and skeletal remains of a cedar cottage.

"This cannot be the right place," said Albert. He looked about dubiously.

The trio stepped gingerly through the ruins. Suddenly, Lavinia gave a petrified cry. Fanning herself vigorously with one hand, she directed the other to a scorched table.

On the table was a sparkling gold coin. Precisely where Albert left it the night before.

The Man Behind Her

Lil and Hy Abramowitz worked for many years at their gentleman's clothing shop in South Elgin and were well-known faces in the community. Eventually, they closed the shop's doors for the final time and retired to a cozy condo, literally steps away from the Fox River. They invited me to visit them there.

I journeyed along Army Trail Road, the former pathway General Winfield Scott's soldiers traversed during the Black Hawk War of 1832. I arrived at the Abramowitz home in late afternoon. Lil ushered me straight to the kitchen, where delicious scents hovered.

"God willing," she said, "we'll live and be well now that we're retired. We'll travel. Spoil our grandchildren. Enjoy life."

"Lil, Lil." Hy chided his wife with good nature. "She doesn't want you should talk about retirement. She wants to hear about your ghost."

"Oh, no," I protested. "I'd love to hear all about your retirement—and your grandchildren, too."

"Here, I decided to make you some matzo ball soup so we could sit and be social. Don't even think about saying no." Lil placed a steaming bowl before me at the table. "Eat. Enjoy."

"When she makes up her mind, you don't argue. Am I right, Lil?" Hy asked.

"You're right, Hy."

Although I hardly knew Lil and Hy Abramowitz—I had only met them a week earlier through a friend of a friend—the couple swarmed around me in parental warmth. After plying me with the tasty soup, half a bagel, and three cookies, Lil settled in to relate her tale.

To officially initiate their retirement, Hy and Lil journeyed to West Dundee to visit a dear friend, Irving Rosen.

With a population under 10,000, West Dundee has retained its charm. One of the town's famous sons is Allan Pinkerton, a Glasgow émigré who initially set up shop as a cooper, or barrel maker. As fate would have it, he crossed paths with a group of counterfeiters, and Pinkerton made his entry into law enforcement. In 1852, he started the Pinkerton Detective Agency, with its infamous "all-seeing eye" logo.

In 1861, Pinkerton foiled a scheme to assassinate President Lincoln; the grateful President asked him to launch the Secret Service.

In today's West Dundee, Irving Rosen lives with his son and daughter-in-law in a grand mansion. The Rosen family converted the estate into a bed and breakfast, and it quickly became quite a popular tourist destination.

"Many times Irv invited us to stay in that B and B," said Lil.

"Many times," Hy agreed.

Lil continued, "After retirement, we finally had the opportunity to take Irv up on his offer. Best of all, it's a pet-friendly B and B, so we got to take along our kitty cat Blossom."

A Victorian painted lady, the plum-colored mansion in West Dundee is adorned with five gables and elaborate gingerbread trim. With a third-story ballroom, a wine cellar, and an inviting wraparound porch, it's a relic from a more refined period.

"It's the kind of house that people drive past for a look-see," said Hy.

"I've been one of those lookers," I confessed.

"It's the kind of house where elegant ladies in hooped skirts and dashing men in tailcoats gathered for lavish parties," said Lil.

Hy said, "If those walls could talk, as they say."

Irving took Lil and Hy Abramowitz on a tour of the magnificent home. He highlighted its original mouldings, stained glass windows, and finely wrought lighting fixtures.

"It's a beauty, all right, but I won't lie," Irving said. "This joint's haunted."

"Haunted!" Lil gasped.

"How do you mean, haunted?" Hy asked.

"Ah, some ghost alarms the guests."

"How do you mean, alarms?" asked Lil.

"It's no big deal. You'll see." Irving shrugged.

"I'll tell you something, Irving, I'm not too sure that I *want* to see. It's bad enough already locals in South Elgin claim that long ago a witch put a curse on our village. They say she still spies on the town from her hovel."

"From her hovel," said Hy.

Lil was getting worked up. "I don't care if I'm in this fancy-schmancy place with gorgeous tile ceilings, plaster walls, and crystal chandeliers. I'm telling you, Irving, I'm not too keen on having a ghost alarm me."

"She's not too keen."

That night, after meeting the other guests, Lil and Hy retired to their four-poster bed. Heads resting on goose-down pillows, they sighed in contentment and kissed each other good night. Despite Lil's admitted trepidation, the night mercifully passed without incident.

"I think that old *meshungana* Irv was just yanking our chains," said Hy in the morning. "He always did have a wacky sense of humor. Are you ready yet, Lil, to go down to the dining room for breakfast? I smell muffins."

"Go, Hy, go. I'll toodle downstairs in just one sec. I need to dab on a smidge of lipstick so I shouldn't frighten the other guests so bright and early in the morning."

Blossom curled around Lil's feet and curiously watched her prepare to greet the day. As Lil buttoned her pink cardigan, she saw from the corner of her eye a black shape flit past.

"I'm plagued with eye floaters, and I often see cloudy shapes in my field of vision. So at first, I didn't think much of the shadow. But I had this creepy sensation that someone was breathing down my neck. My back felt a wispy movement, like someone brushed right against it."

"Right against it," said Hy.

"I turned around a few times to check, but there was no one there."

"There was no one there."

Lil went on, "Our Blossom was restless, too. Her body stiffened and her fur stood on end. The poor kitty was all puffed up like a Halloween cat."

In her room at the Rosens' B and B, Lil bent to pat Blossom's head.

"It's all right, dolly," she said and stood up again with some effort.

"Bad knees," said Hy.

Lil opened the narrow closet door, which contained a full-length mirror inside. She fluffed her handsome silver hair and dotted on her lipstick.

Directly behind her in the mirror, close enough that she could feel his breath, a tall man with a handlebar mustache adjusted his striped vest.

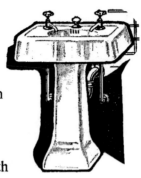

Lil whirled around. She and Blossom were alone. Her heart in her throat, Lil twisted toward the mirror again. The man behind her tramped to the washbasin and smoothed his hair with a minty tonic.

"I could smell the mint."

"She could smell it."

"You can see that I'm a senior citizen. I'm 70, but I bolted downstairs as if I were a sprightly girl of 10."

"Oy, what a commotion she raised," said Hy. "She was screaming like a banshee and was as white as a sheet. I'm telling you, her hair was standing on end."

"On end," said Lil.

"She had Blossom clutched to her chest, and they both looked like they had seen a ghost."

"We *had* seen a ghost! I refused to spend one more second in that house where cockamamie spirits sneak up behind you and breathe down your neck when you're trying to put on a smidge of color."

"When she makes up her mind, you don't argue. Am I right, Lil?"

"You're right, Hy."

"Now, I ask you, can you think of any rational reason for my alarming experience in that room?" Lil demanded.

I honestly tried, but I failed to conjure up one plausible explanation.

Hy and Lil's story has remained with me daily. Each time I glance in the mirror, I find myself checking for more than a presentable appearance.

Augusta's Diamond Ring

One of the most bizarre bits of St. Charles' history is the notorious Richards' Riot of 1849. It took place at the home of Dr. George Richards, founder of the Franklin Medical College, Illinois' first medical school.

For seven years the college prospered, until John Rood, a misguided student, learned of the premature death of 16-year-old Marilla Kenyon and concocted a grisly scheme. Only recently married, the teenager succumbed to cholera; her family buried her near their home east of Sycamore. However, ill-fated Marilla was not allowed, initially, to rest in peace.

John Rood was hell bent on snatching the body for his educational edification. In short, he wanted a cadaver for dissection and study. Rood journeyed to the Sycamore area, stole Marilla's body from her grave, and stashed her corpse in Dr. Richards' barn.

Marilla's disconsolate family soon learned of the bodysnatching and connected it to Franklin Medical College. An outraged and gun-wielding posse, lead by Marilla's husband, stormed St. Charles to confront Dr. Richards. Although he denied knowledge of the grave robbery, Dr. Richards was wounded when the angry mob blasted bullets through the door of his home. A gunshot wound to the head killed John Rood, and Marilla was eventually returned to her rightful resting place.

That same year, a related incident occurred in neighboring La Fox.

Caleb Squint was an acknowledged miser. He lived a life of monetary abundance, which he closely guarded, and emotional scarcity. Cosseted in his fine warm home, he shut his eyes against those in need. He shook his head in annoyance at any who sought a bite to eat, a piece of coal, a friendly face. Scowling, he turned them away into the cold.

Now, one day Caleb Squint decided to take a wife. He journeyed far and wide to find a woman who owned as much as he. It was not an easy quest for Squint, for women were notoriously lacking in property in those days. Yet, let it not be said that Squint was an indolent man. Driven by dreams of greater wealth, he obsessively pursued his mission.

Eventually, he met a wealthy widow with two bright sons and took her for his wife. Augusta was jolly and industrious and intelligent; but Squint cared not for these attributes. Instead, he coveted the sizeable diamond ring, a family heirloom, which sparkled on her plump index finger.

When several La Fox families where stricken with cholera in 1849, Augusta rushed to their aid. She tirelessly nursed the sick until she too fell ill.

Robust and spirited, Augusta radiated life. Caleb Squint, naturally, was stunned when cholera claimed her—flabbergasted really, for Augusta seemed a veritable force of nature. Someone whose presence would surely be eternal.

For the funeral, Squint selected his most somber clothing from what was a somber wardrobe indeed. Upon his narrow face he affixed his gravest scowl. Nevertheless, despite his best efforts at impersonating a grieving husband, all Squint could contemplate was Augusta's diamond ring, glittering on her cold, dead finger.

"We must remove your mother's ring posthaste. Before she is buried," Caleb Squint said to his stepsons. "She would surely want us to keep it in her memory."

"No, no," cried Augusta's mournful boys. "The ring must stay with Mama, for she loves it dearly. It will light her way through eternity."

Squint scowled. "Pshaw! It's an utter crime to allow a treasure such as that diamond to remain in the cold, dark ground."

"No, no. The ring must stay with Mama. It will provide warmth, protect Mama from the gloom of her grave."

Undeterred and under cover of darkness, Squint stole to the graveyard beside the house. Panting with his efforts, he exhumed Augusta's body and wrestled to pull the ring from her finger. Alas, it was tightly fixed. With a few snips, Squint cut away the finger with the sharp shears he carried with him. He plunked the unwanted finger into the casket and pocketed Augusta's diamond ring. Hastily, he reburied the coffin.

More content than he had ever been, Caleb Squint returned to the warmth of his bed. His face was stamped with—could it be?—his best attempt at a smile. Squint slipped the diamond ring under his pillow and dreamed of the riches it would bring.

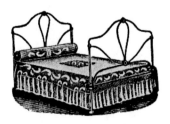

What was that? Was he dreaming? From the graveyard beside the house, Squint heard a distant tapping from within the coffin.

Tap, tap, tap.

He heard the woeful wail of a strident voice, which howled around his home like an Arctic wind. Squint jerked his head from the pillow.

"Who's there?" he called. Silence.

"Pshaw! I caught a bit of chill at the graveyard and it has encroached upon my slumber."

Squint rested against the pillow once more, his lids heavy. At his front door, he heard a staccato tapping, like a raven pecking at the wood.

Tap, tap, tap.

The shrill voice roared once more. From the bottom of the stairway, Squint heard its yowl reverberating.

"Whooooo?"

Squint's teeth clanked in terror. Trembling, he pulled the bedclothes above his head.

Closer, now, up the stairs, the voice intoned, "Whooooo?"

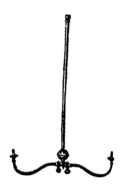

Squint heard footsteps—dragging footsteps—upon the stairs. Laboriously, they drew nearer.

Quaking so violently that he could scarcely hold the bedcovers in place, Caleb Squint screamed, "Who's there? Who comes this way?"

Augusta, blue-tinged and raging, drifted through the door. She wrenched the quilts from the bed.

"Whooooo has my diamond riiiiing?"

Gripping the severed finger in her hands, she pointed it at Squint, who could find no saliva to flush away the panic in his gullet. His quivering body nearly tumbled from the bed. His throat was raw, his voice a rasp.

"I—I—do not know who has taken your diamond ring. I swear it."

"Whooooo has my diamond riiiiing? Whooooo?"

Augusta crept onto the foot of the bed. The draft of the tomb enveloped Squint. He spied puffs of his own breath in the icy bedchamber as he gasped, "I—I—swear—"

Squint leaned back against his frosty pillow, his body rattling like a skeleton.

As Augusta howled, Squint gazed into her maw, cavernous and foreboding. She tapped the severed finger against Squint's bony chest.

Tap, tap, tap.

"Whooooo has my diamond riiiiing? Whooooo has my diamond riiiiing?"

Augusta snaked her arm toward Squint's pillow. Directly under his bulging eyes, the severed finger led the way.

"Take your bloody ring, take it!
Begone! I beseech you!" Squint
hurled the wretched ring toward
Augusta.

Scowling, he turned her away into
the cold.

Radiant in the brightness of her
diamond ring, Augusta floated out
the window.

A veritable force of nature, she vowed to visit Squint the
following evening and every evening after that.

Tap, tap, tap.

Aurora Borealis

On a dismal November night in 1931, a few days after Halloween, Harry and Ruth Lyons strolled home from an evening at the talking pictures. They had seen the premiere of *Frankenstein,* starring Boris Karloff in the mute role of Frankenstein's monster.

"That theatre takes my breath away," Ruth said. "It's gorgeous, just gorgeous."

The Paramount Theatre, newly opened in Aurora, was a unique combination of Venetian and Art Deco styling. Inside, its hand-painted murals, with rich, lavish colors, depicted gondoliers and *commedia dell'arte* figures. Ruth, an art major, found them particularly intriguing.

"How about the movie? That took your breath away, too. You were gasping to beat the band," said Harry. He balanced his umbrella carefully over their heads, shielding them from the misty drizzle.

Ruth watched much of the film through her fingers, which she splayed across her eyes to distance herself from the huge screen and her own fear.

"Did you take me to a scary movie on purpose so I'd keep burying my face in your shoulder?" she asked.

"Am I that transparent?" laughed Harry. "Remember when we saw *Dracula* on Valentine's Day? You practically crawled under the theatre seat."

"I keep waiting for a bat to fly through our window…. But, really, I felt so sorry for Frankenstein's monster."

"Felt sorry for him? Are you serious? If you ask me, you seemed terrified of the big lug."

"Well, at first I was," Ruth admitted. "Then I came to understand that the poor creature just wanted a bit of companionship."

"Companionship, eh? Just needed a friend, did he?"

"Yes, as we all do."

A sudden gust of wind lurched the umbrella backward, as if someone were yanking it from Harry's hand. He struggled to right it.

"That was weird," he said. "I just felt something flit past me. Like a bat."

"You're just trying to scare me," laughed Ruth. "Harry, do you think it's possible? Life after death, I mean."

"Nah, it's not possible. When your number's up, it's up."

"You don't think there's another realm? Something more than Heaven and Earth?"

"Nope, I don't. I'm a card-carrying cynic."

"I thought you were a photographer."

"That too."

Ruth, pensive, said, "I think there's got to be another state of being—souls still among us, pursuing unfinished business or unrequited love. Or addressing other loose ends still nagging at them from the grave."

"We have to agree to disagree on this one," said Harry. "But I promise, if I do come back to haunt you someday, I won't do it as a scarred monster with bolts in my neck."

"Thanks, Mr. Cynic. I do appreciate that."

The rain began to fall more heavily. Hurrying, Harry and Ruth turned onto Dove Street and headed toward their four-flat.

"Harry, we forgot to turn the lights off," Ruth said, noting a glow through a gap in the curtains of their second-floor bedroom window.

"Funny," Harry thought, with a trickle of alarm. "I'm certain I checked all the lights before we left."

"Guess we're just contributing to the city's overall luminosity," he said aloud. Aurora, one of the first cities in the United States to use electric streetlights, was dubbed "The City of Lights" in 1908.

"Well, we were in a real hurry to make the show."

As Harry glanced at the window again, he thought he noticed the curtain shift—a nearly imperceptible flicker. As if someone were peeking out at them.

"I'm letting *Frankenstein* get to me," he thought.

At their flat, Harry slid his key into the door and held it open for Ruth. He shook out his umbrella.

"Come into my laboratory," he said. "Mwwwahhh, ha, ha!"

"Stop, you!" cried Ruth, stepping into the front room. "You're making me nervous. Why don't I pour us some sherry? We'll listen to the radio. I need to get that unfortunate monster out of my mind."

"Sounds great. Let me go turn off the bedroom lights real quick. No sense running up the electric bill."

Still clutching the umbrella, Harry took a few quick steps down the hallway.

"That's peculiar," he thought. "I don't remember closing the bedroom door when we left."

His hand rested lightly on the crystal doorknob. He felt uneasy. On edge. Something wasn't quite right. Could there be an intruder within?

Adrenaline placed him on high alert. His heart raced, and his muscles tensed expectantly.

Cautiously, he opened the door—just a crack. Stillness greeted him. Pushing the door further, he placed one foot into the hushed bedroom. The room was dark, the lamps unlit. Had the intruder heard Harry and shut the lights?

Hurriedly, Harry flipped the light switch. For a moment, he listened, eyes closed in concentration. Then he peered to and fro. He noticed nothing unusual, but something felt different. He couldn't quite put his finger on it....

Positive he had seen a light from the street, he crouched, peering beneath the bed. He sprawled out, flattening himself to squeeze partially under the bed frame and deeply regretting the second helping of mashed potatoes and gravy he had eaten for dinner.

He cleared his throat and prepared to yell for Ruth to run from the flat.

Using the umbrella as a probe, Harry poked it under the bed and swung it back and forth. One of Ruth's pink-feathered mules flew out, a glob of dust marring the slipper's quilted satin surface.

He heard a muffled fluttering behind him and banged his head on the mattress. From within the closet, a skittering, a faint hissing.

"Good Lord, there's an animal in there," he thought, simultaneously irritated and relieved. "How did it get in?"

Stealthily, Harry rose. He filled his lungs and tiptoed toward the closet. A thin splinter of light gleamed from its keyhole. Louder grew the noises from within.

Harry closed in on the animal—a squirrel? a starling? God, not a bat— that had taken up residence there. He brandished the umbrella, his soggy shield, and opened the closet door.

A brilliant orb bounced toward him and grazed his cheek. It drifted through the plaster wall and into the hallway.

"Uh!" Startled, Harry swayed. He steadied himself and bolted out the bedroom door in pursuit of the ball of white light. His umbrella a makeshift weapon, Harry charged into the front room.

There stood Ruth, paralyzed with fright, her fingers splayed across her face like a Venetian mask. The orb fluttered around her head and twirled beneath her elbows.

"Ruth! Keep still, Honey," hissed Harry.

"Is it a bat?"

"No, it's a— I don't know exactly...."

"C-c-catch it. Or open the windows and let it out."

"Not before I take its picture," thought Harry. He crept toward his camera on the writing desk and seized it. The umbrella clattered to the floor.

The luminous ball hovered over Ruth's impeccably arranged finger waves, while Harry, his arms wobbly, struggled to aim his camera.

"Why won't my fingers cooperate?" he thought. "They're tense, so tense." They felt as though they might crack off.

The glowing orb drifted above Ruth, seemingly content to wait for Harry to snap a photograph. At last, Harry steadied his hands and forced his unyielding fingers to give way.

As he took a picture, the ball of light faded, shrank a bit. It released a slight hiss.

Gingerly, Harry tapped the orb with the tip of the umbrella, scarcely making contact with it. He directed it toward the window. With a sizzle, the orb dissolved.

Behind her fingers, Ruth opened one eye.

"Is it gone?" she whispered.

"It evaporated," Harry whispered back. "Why are we whispering?"

"I need to whisper for now. Where's that sherry?"

They searched the front room for signs that the ball of light had been present, but they could find none.

"Harry, you will never—I repeat—*never* get me to watch a scary movie again," Ruth announced.

"Don't you worry," he said. "I have no desire...."

"Those things I said about other realms—I'm sorry I ever mentioned them."

"No, I'm the one who's sorry. This card-carrying cynic is ripping up his card."

When Harry developed the photo, it revealed within the orb a face in profile, with a slim nose and prominent cheekbones. It appeared to be grinning.

Harry wanted to give the bizarre photo to his editor at the newspaper where he worked, but Ruth insisted that they keep it to themselves. Whoever it was just wanted a bit of companionship, she argued, before the night whisked it away. No sense scaring the whole city.

Exhausted, they finally crawled into bed. Harry shut out the lights—but not before he tucked the umbrella under the bed. Just in case.

Don't Make Me Come Down There

"Don't make me come down there," Renata Johansson called to her children in the basement of their Elgin home.

She hunched at the kitchen table, poured over the doctor bills, and wondered how in the world she was going to stretch the meatloaf one more day. Against the wall, the cast iron radiator wheezed. She would have to call the landlord again.

Outside the window of her cottage, crafted with stones from the Fox River, Renata saw the enormous Elgin National Watch Company clock tower looming in the distance. Its presence provided a sense of constancy that Renata craved in the face of her life's general upheaval. Recently divorced from her husband Ronald, she was trekking over the uncharted territory of single parenthood, an unusual situation for a woman in 1947.

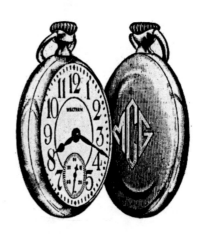

In the basement, 12-year-old Ray and 6-year-old Patsy argued vociferously. Their voices, piercing and irritated, echoed through the floor.

"Mom," Ray yelled. "Puh-*leeze!* Tell her to stop bothering me."

"*He's* the one bothering *me*," cried Patsy. "He's standing in the middle of my play kitchen."

Sighing, Renata pushed aside her bills and strode to the basement landing. She called down, "Ray, Patsy, the basement's big enough for both of you. You need to cooperate."

Ray protested, "I'm trying to do my science project, and Patsy's getting her big face my way."

"I was here first. Me 'n' Lulabelle 'n' Mr. Frogface are having a tea party."

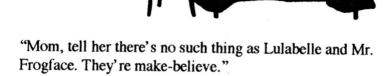

"Mom, tell her there's no such thing as Lulabelle and Mr. Frogface. They're make-believe."

"There is *too* such a thing! Lulabelle and Mr. Frogface are my friends!" shrieked Patsy.

"Come upstairs please, Ray," Renata said. "Now."

He thundered upstairs and plopped at the table.

"You called?"

"Ray, I need you to stop bickering with your sister. You're nearly a teenager—twice Patsy's age. You're the man of the house now, and I'm counting on you to cooperate."

"Mom, I need to finish my science project, but Patsy keeps—"

"The volcano?"

"Yep, I'm building a volcano that really erupts for the science fair."

"Sounds interesting."

"Mom, you're trying to change the subject. Patsy's clanking around all those little teacups and saucers Grandma gave her."

"Ray, try to place yourself in Patsy's position."

"How?"

"Think about what it must be like for Patsy. She's cooped up inside with the chicken pox—pun intended. She's feeling itchy and cranky. On top of that, she's removed from her usual routine, away from all her friends."

"Just 'cuz she has the Bubonic Plague doesn't mean she can plague me."

"Don't you remember, Ray, how miserable it was to have chicken pox? You scratched incessantly."

"Aw, Mom, that was a million years ago. But I still have the crater it left next to my ear." He lifted his hair. "See?"

Renata nodded and lightly touched the scar.

"I even had those little buggers in my eyes and ears, remember? I had to flush my ol' eyeballs out every single day. It makes me prickly just to think about it."

Ray twitched and scratched himself with an exaggerated motion as Renata chuckled, a pleasant release from the stress she labored to conceal from the children. Fretting about her long hours as a legal secretary, about imposing on her mother to assist her with childcare, and now about Patsy's chicken pox, Renata felt like the juggler of massive pins. At any moment, she feared, they could come crashing down to flatten her.

"I can't wait 'til Patsy goes back to school and has her girlfriends to play with again," Ray said.

"Dr. Khoury told me that Patsy could go back to school next week. The worst of it's behind her now. We're just waiting for all the blisters to dry."

"Bleccch," said Ray. *"Those* eruptions are totally repulsive. Not dramatic like my volcano. I don't know how Patsy stands to look at herself in the mirror. And she reeks of calamine lotion!"

"What did I just say about placing yourself in Patsy's position? This is tough on her."

"She keeps prattling on and on to Lulabelle and Mr. Frogface. I can't hear myself think!"

"I'm going downstairs to let Patsy know that it's bath time. Can I recruit you to make meatloaf sandwiches and pack lunches for tomorrow? Then, the basement's all yours."

"Sure. Want me to make a couple sandwiches for Patsy and Grandma, too?"

"That's my thoughtful young man."

Pulling her sweater tightly across her chest, Renata descended the few steps into the chilly basement.

"Hi, Sweetie. How's the tea party?"

"Real good," said Patsy.

Wearing a pink tutu over her pajamas, her faced dotted with angry blisters, Patsy sat at the tiny table Ronald had built for her a year earlier. With miniature cups and saucers and a child-sized teapot, the table was set for four.

"Which guests are joining you tonight?" asked Renata.

"Here's Mr. Frogface eating his banana cream pie. He's all dressed up in his new top hat. See?" Patsy gestured to the chair beside her, then tilted her chin toward the toy kitchen set. "Lulabelle's over there. At the stove. She's making more food for Mr. Frogface."

Renata grinned, noting the toy frying pan and plastic bacon on the stovetop.

"Smells good. Now, let's tell everyone goodnight, Sweetie. It's time to go upstairs and take your nice oatmeal bath. It'll soothe that pesky itching."

"Can we tuck my friends in first?" asked Patsy. She stood and scratched her tummy. Shuffling in her bunny slippers, Patsy reached the petite wooden bed Ronald had built for her and pulled back its woolly covers.

"Climb in, Lulabelle. You too, Mr. Frogface. Nighty night." Patsy tucked the blanket around her imaginary playmates. "Tell 'em goodnight, Mom."

"Nighty night, don't let the bedbugs bite. All right, Sweetie Pie. Bath time."

Renata and Patsy returned to the kitchen, where Ray was mass-producing sandwiches like an automaton. He squirted ketchup over the first, forming his initials, and moved along to the next.

"Don't give me the crust, okay?" said Patsy.

"I won't, Patsy. I'm making you my super duper extra special meatloaf sammich. Gotta try to get your appetite back, you know."

"Extra special? Yum."

Relief flood Renata. "Ray really is a good kid," she thought. "I knew I could count on him.

"Yep," said Ray. "This super special sammich is guaranteed to make even the poxiest pox person feel like—"

From the basement echoed the clattering of a miniature teacup being replaced in its saucer.

Ray, with the ketchup bottle suspended over a slice of bread and with his mouth forming a perfect circle, froze.

"What was that?" Renata stiffened.

"Aw, that's jus' Scooter," said Patsy.

"Scooter?" Ray and Renata asked.

Trotting to the basement landing, Patsy called, "Scooter, I told you, it's time for bed. Don't make me come down there!"

Just a Big Kid at Heart

Clark Hallowell of East Dundee was just a big kid at heart. Sure, he had a wife and four-year-old twins, Mary Kate and Stevie—precious responsibilities—yet, they only added to his merry band of playmates.

Almost as much as he adored his family, Clark cherished his electric train set. Passed from one foster home to another as a child, Clark eyed with open envy the toys of his chums. One day, he promised himself, one day I'll have a train set, too.

Slowly acquired piece by treasured piece in his adulthood, the train now circled the Christmas tree in the Hallowell home. Its *clickety-clack* provided a constant metronome for the festive tunes Clark's wife Shirley stacked on the hi-fi and blared throughout the apartment.

Clark reveled in the hustle and bustle of the holiday season, the sense of expectation, the picture-postcard dusting of powdery snow. With a spring in his step on that Christmas Eve, he headed out of the accountant's firm where he was employed—a necessary responsibility—and boarded the train for home.

Clutching an overhead strap, Clark daydreamed. He gently smiled, half asleep, as he anticipated his arrival in his apartment. Shirley would hail him with a kiss. The twins would ride atop his feet, would cling to his legs as he laughingly attempted, without success, to remove his topcoat.

Later in the evening Clark and the kids would gather for their after-dinner holiday tradition. Crouched on their knees and cupping their chins in their palms, Stevie and Mary Kate huddled under the Christmas tree. Above their heads, bubble lights fizzed from their perches on the fir branches. Behind them, Clark squeezed their little feet—clad in Dr. Denton jammies—once, twice, three times. It never failed to prompt gleeful giggles.

"Ready, set, go!" Clark would say. Then he'd throw the switch to set the train in motion. *Clickety-clack! Clickety-clack!*

"Yay!" Mary Kate and Stevie would squeal.

Deep in his reverie, Clark thought, "I'm a lucky man. A lucky man."

It was his final reflection, for at that moment the train on which he rode slammed into a stalled car, catapulted into the air, and somersaulted, landing on its top side. Clark Hallowell, devoted family man and big kid at heart, lost his life on the tracks.

Listening to the radio at home, Shirley learned of the train wreck. Filled with a deathly calm, she knew; she just knew. A primordial awareness gripped her as she phoned her parents.

By the time the police officers arrived to inform Shirley of Clark's death, her parents, with gamely slapped on grins that failed to touch their hollow eyes, were playing with the twins.

Mary Kate's and Stevie's eyes may have been on their toys, but their ears were otherwise engaged. Mary Kate's shriek interrupted Shirley's hushed conversation with the officers.

"Daddy's dead!"

Despite their soothing words and ample laps, Shirley's parents could not comfort the children, whose cries grew gasping and whose chests raggedly heaved. Surreptitiously, Shirley beckoned her mother.

"I refuse, I simply refuse to forever link Christmas with Clark's death," Shirley whispered urgently. "Clark would want us to conduct ourselves as we ordinarily do."

She resolutely gathered the twins into her arms.

"Daddy wants us to turn on the train, as we do every night."

"No!" Stevie stomped his foot. "Not without Daddy."

"Nuh-uh." Mary Kate shook her head and fisted her hands at her waist.

Shirley's eyes ached. She longed to crumble, to allow herself to tumble into the quicksand of her despair. Almost imperceptibly, she nodded to her parents and pressed against the swinging door to the kitchen. Like a rag doll, she collapsed at the Formica table and buried her head in her arms, soundlessly weeping.

Clark's tender hand seemed to massage her arm, the back of her neck. His touch was palpable. Shirley jerked her head up. She expected to see him beside her, to learn that it was all a hideous nightmare, a terrible mistake. But Clark wasn't there.

Clickety-clack! Clickety-clack! The train whirred into motion from the living room.

"Yay!" Mary Kate and Stevie cried.

Immensely relieved, Shirley stood on unsteady legs and returned to her family. Hunkered down on their knees, eyes glistening with joy, the twins silently watched the train race around the tree. Bubble lights effervesced over their heads.

"Thank goodness," Shirley murmured to her parents. "Which one turned it on?"

Brows furrowed, Shirley's parents glanced from Shirley to the train and back.

"We thought you did," said Shirley's dad.

"There's only one switch, and it's in this room," Shirley said. "Kids, which one of you turned on the train?"

Stevie said, "Daddy did. Right after he squeezed our feet—one, two, three. Like he always does."

A dedicated family man and a big kid at heart, Clark joined his merry band of playmates one last time that Christmas Eve.

Today, Steve and Mary Kate are all grown up, with families of their own. Whenever Mary Kate unpacks the holiday decorations, she cradles an old bubble light in her palms, reminiscing. As Steve assembles the train beneath his tree, he feels the same exquisite anticipation he felt years ago, waiting for Daddy to come home from work.

Steve and Mary Kate trim their Christmas trees and flip the switches on their electric trains. they feel Clark's playful presence. Their children loll in delight to watch the trains race over bridges and through snow banks. Behind them, Steve and Mary Kate squeeze their little feet.

A reassuring gesture that connects Christmas Past and Present.

Sky's the Limit

"Why so glum, chum?" Alice Hoffstedder of Waukesha inquired when she encountered her nine-year-old grandson Marc listlessly flipping through a weighty encyclopedia.

"Aw, Gram, I'm bummed out," Marc said.

"Why so bummed, chum?"

"I have to write a report on early aviators."

"That's a fascinating, inspirational topic. Why would it make you blue?"

Marc, eyes blazing with urgency, asked, "Do you swear on stack of Bibles not to repeat what I'm going to tell you?"

"I swear," Alice said, forming a cross over her heart.

"See, my teacher said to parachute into my research and collect—what was it? Oh, yeah, 'interesting facts and memorable details.'"

"Sounds like a capital plan."

"Don't tell anyone, Gram, but I don't read too good," Marc divulged. His slight shoulders slumped. "Now do you think I'm your dumb chum?"

"Never, Marc. We all learn differently and have individual strengths and weaknesses. For example, I may be a crackerjack reader, but I can't tally a column of numbers to save my soul."

"Sheesh, I'll never figure out what all these long words mean. The short ones are tough, too. I found these neat old pictures, though."

"One can never underestimate the value of a rousing visual," Alice proclaimed. "Your photographs are a solid start to your research."

"I guess…" Marc shrugged, unconvinced.

"Marc David Hoffstedder, do *you* swear on a stack of Bibles that you won't tell anyone what *I'm* about to reveal?"

"I swear." Marc extended his pinky finger and interlocked it with Alice's in a solemn oath of secrecy.

"I can share an unparalleled visual with you. A homemade plane that the Waukesha Flying Club used decades ago in their air shows."

"Homemade?"

"Yes, indeedy! As homemade as my celebrated boysenberry pie. My old friend Duke Klein sent away for a mail-order plane kit back in 1929. For a whole summer, he tinkered and tweaked until he constructed a dandy two-seater in his father's barn. "

"In 1929? That was 40 years ago—and the plane's still around?"

"Yes, and I'll bet we can even coax Daredevil Duke to take to the skies for us."

"Wow!" said Marc.

"Fly that pinky finger again, chum, and shake with me to ensure that you never refer to yourself as dumb again. Good! Now, dive into your jacket, please. Let's make like a tree and leaf."

As they drove, Marc peppered Alice with questions.

"Who's Duke? Where does he live? Is he an aviator?"

"Duke was part of a fearless passel of upstarts that ushered in a new sport—barnstorming. Those daredevil stunt pilots risked life and limb to entertain folks across the Midwest."

"What's a stunt pilot?" Marc asked.

"Why, they performed death-defying aerial acrobatics for mesmerized crowds. I was lucky enough to be one of the extremely exhilarated people who cheered them."

"What acrobatics did they do?"

"They executed loop the loops, figure eights, and barrel rolls in the sky. Pilots flew wobbly gliders so low that those contraptions grazed barn roofs—hence, the term *barnstormers.*"

"I get it now."

"Dashing daredevils, gussied up in flowing white scarves, leapt from one speeding plane to another. My daddy used to say it turned his hair white just to *think* of those perilous exploits."

"What stunts did Duke perform?"

"Daredevil Duke was known far and wide for—well, I won't *tell* you just yet. Let's see if we can wheedle Duke into *showing* you."

"Isn't he a real old codger now? Like, your age?"

"I beg your pardon," Alice snorted indignantly.

"Sorry, Gram. I mean, is he still able to do tricks and all?"

"You be the judge of that," Alice said. She stopped her vehicle in a field beside a towering barn with wood so weathered it proved difficult to discern against the gray sky. Behind his wire-rimmed glasses, Marc squinted to bring the barn into sharper focus, noting that at its entry rested a Pietenpol Air Camper. He bolted from the car and raced to the plane.

"This is *so* cool!"

"Daredevil Duke constructed this plane of spruce and plywood. It's held together with Casein glue and powered by a Ford Model A engine. How do you like *that* for memorable details?"

"I like it, I like it," Marc laughed.

Alice checked her watch.

"If I'm not mistaken, Duke should be along any minute," she said, pointing upward. "Listen...."

On command, a red and white biplane roared overhead. It buzzed the top of the barn and dove so low to the ground that Marc clearly spotted the argyle sweater peeking from the top of Duke's leather bomber jacket. His eyes concealed behind goggles, Duke blew a kiss to Alice and saluted Marc.

Marc cheered as the plane soared across the field and staged a series of loop the loops. He hooted in approval as it back-flipped and glided upside down before spinning unhurriedly to an upright position.

With his co-pilot at the controls, Duke removed his safety belt and acrobatically swung onto the upper wing. Arms outstretched theatrically and silk scarf flapping behind him, he sauntered from one wing tip to the other.

Alice nudged Marc. "That elegant stroll is called wing walking. It's Duke's warm-up before his famous finish."

Marc gasped as Duke performed a handstand, righted himself, and flamboyantly bowed. Then, Duke dexterously dangled by his feet from the lower wing as the biplane darted over the barn and vroomed out of sight.

"What showmanship," Alice marveled, her eyes misty. "Duke's death was the ultimate irony."

"His *death?*" Marc cried. "Gram, what are you talkin' about?"

"One flawlessly clear morning, Duke and his co-pilot were scoping out a field where they were to perform the next day. Duke unhooked his seatbelt. He leaned out of the plane to inspect the terrain below. At that instant, the co-pilot lost control of the plane, and it flipped like a quarter in a coin toss. Daredevil Duke, my dear friend, tumbled to his death in a dreadful freak accident."

"But I don't get it—he was just *here*." Marc scanned the vast heavens.

Alice explained, "Duke may be gone, but his spirit lives on. And I believe you know what I mean by *spirit*. Now, pop those eyeballs back into your skull, chum. You have a report to write. I think we can make sense of those troublesome words when we harken back to the visuals Duke so graciously provided, eh?"

"Sky's the limit, Gram!"

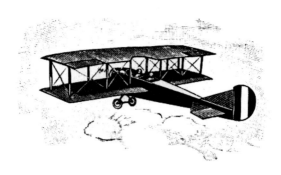

The Swimmin' Hole

Kayla Kinsey, a new resident of Burlington, had not yet mingled enough with us locals to know that the swimmin' hole was strictly off limits. Several days after she moved into our neck of the woods, I trotted over to her place with a bowl of my Pleased-Ta-Meetcha Potato Salad, intending to warn her.

Regrettably, I missed Kayla by fifteen minutes. By the time I knocked on her door, she was already perfecting her breaststroke at the swimmin' hole.

Back in 1957, when I was just knee-high to a badger, the schoolyard bully, Buster Normandt, drowned in the swimmin' hole. After his death, kids claimed that Buster's corpse contaminated the water, prompted pink eye outbreaks, and introduced a bewildering bacterium that eradicated the blue-winged teal population.

Once a watery playground, the swimmin' hole no longer held appeal; to this day, in fact, we townies avoid it like the plague.

It's no wonder kids blamed Buster for any evils that befell us. Ya, you betcha, Buster was a despicable character. Actually made my blood curdle. Buster possessed that loathsome knack of being able to microscopically hone in on a person's unique vulnerabilities. Then, he'd pounce at the jugular and rip his patsy's throat out, preferably in front of an audience.

I was one of Buster's targets. He christened me "Two-Ton Tessie," and whenever I sprawled on my beach towel, he chortled, "Beached whale!" Hurt my feelings somethin' fierce.

"Run for your lives!" Buster bellowed, one morning when I belly-flopped off the fixed raft at the swimmin' hole. "Tidal wave!"

He doubled over, guffawing, while the other kids uneasily shifted their weight and glanced over the waves, avoiding my wounded eyes. My cheeks blazed as crimson as the cruel marks the waves imprinted on my skin, a souvenir of shame.

Still stings when I call to mind the memory of that victimization, even though it occurred a lifetime ago.

Now, Kayla, in contrast, she's a
smile-inducer—such a sweet gal.
Works as a dental hygienist down at
Dr. Mason's office and sells her
beautiful pottery over in Lake
Geneva on the weekends. Sure wish
I coulda given her a heads up before
she hopped into that swimmin'
hole....

She took the fateful plunge on July
13, 1995, in the midst of a god-awful
heat wave. Temperatures hovered
over the 100-degree mark and
double-dared folks to come out and
play. Once people ventured outdoors,
the weather captured 'em in a
headlock and tried to smother 'em.
Why, that killer heat wave was directly responsible
for the deaths of nearly 150 people in Wisconsin.

Kayla, she didn't know any better, so she headed to the
swimmin' hole to dodge the suffocating weather. She tightened
her ponytail, kicked off her Keds, and waded into the water up
to her waist.

Briskly kicking away the seaweed that clung to her ankle,
Kayla swam toward the raft that bobbed in the restless waves.
She quickly discovered that it was further away than
anticipated. In time, she lolled on her back, catching her breath
and narrowing her eyes against the punishing sun.

Beneath her, a darting bluegill tickled her heels, and she dropped her legs in surprise. Vigorously treading water, Kayla estimated the remaining distance to the raft.

Without warning, something seized her ankle in a vise-grip clench and tugged mightily, yanking her entire body underwater.

It was not seaweed.

Thrashing wildly beneath the waves, Kayla came face to face with a husky adolescent, his bloated body a mottled purple, his blue lips grinning over algae-crusted teeth. Flailing in panic, she gouged his lifeless eyes and jabbed his distended belly. She launched toward the surface. Beneath her, the boy grasped Kayla's calf, dragging her toward the bottom like an alligator wrestling its prey. Kayla released her jaw in an impotent scream and inhaled the swimmin' hole's foul waters.

"I'm going to die here," she thought, wriggling desperately.

With her free leg, she kicked the grappler's head; stunned, he released her, and Kayla propelled herself to the surface. Coughing violently and racked with spasms, she spewed foamy sputum into the air.

"Dead, dead, dead," she thought, bobbing in the waves.

By then, word reached me that one of the ladies in my bridge club had seen Kayla wading at the swimmin' hole earlier that day. My husband Louie and I broke every speed law in town to reach Kayla, and you'll be pleased to know that Two-Ton Tessie helped pull her to shore and clear her lungs.

I'll never revisit that vile swimmin' hole; nor will Kayla. Ya, you betcha, we locals know—the swimmin' hole's strictly off limits.

Epilogue

Those wee handprints on Wilbur Hawking's car—could they possibly be those of ghostly children who lost their lives, as did that big kid, Clark Hallowell, on the train tracks?

Speaking of Clark, how was it that he managed to join his merry band of playmates for a final flip of the electric train's switch?

In death, Eulalia Buckthorn gained the freedom to roam that was denied her in life. Does she currently protect those who live in the home where she was once held captive?

And Augusta Squint, wagging her severed finger—might she still watch over the land where her husband hastily exhumed, robbed, and reburied her body?

What—or who— was the mysteriously luminescent orb that greeted Harry and Ruth when they returned home after seeing *Frankenstein?*

Could it truly have been Buster Normandt, the long-dead schoolyard bully, who attempted to drown Kayla Kinsey in Burlington's swimmin' hole?

They fill us with questions, these spirits of the Fox Valley, as they reach out to us from days gone by.

Perhaps some of us have heard friends and family members describe ghostly encounters in hushed tones. Although some completely doubt their existence, others remain convinced that spirits of the past still walk among us. The believers maintain that ghosts assist us in times of need, seek vengeance when they have been wronged, and tend to unfinished issues.

The Fox River flows for over 170 miles through Illinois and Wisconsin. Along the charming towns of its historic Fox Valley are mysteries that we may never know or fully comprehend, are sights that, as Zosia Mucha says, "defy reality."

Perhaps these stories of those who have passed on will keep us connected to our heritage along the glorious Fox River.

Index

W

To Order Copies

Please send me _____ copies of *Ghosts of the Fox River Valley* at $9.95 each plus $3.00 S/H. (Make checks payable to Quixote Press.)

Name _____

Street _____

City _____ State _____ Zip _____

QUIXOTE PRESS
3544 Blakslee Street
Wever IA 52658
1-800-571-2665

To Order Copies

Please send me _____ copies of *Ghosts of the Fox River Valley* at $9.95 each plus $3.00 S/H. (Make checks payable to Quixote Press.)

Name _____

Street _____

City _____ State _____ Zip _____

QUIXOTE PRESS
3544 Blakslee Street
Wever IA 52658
1-800-571-2665